Pasefika
The Festival of Pacific Arts

Floyd K. Takeuchi

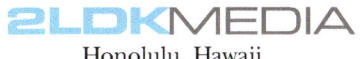
Honolulu, Hawaii

Pasefika
The Festival of Pacific Arts
By Floyd K. Takeuchi

Published by 2LDK Media, Honolulu, Hawaii

ISBN: 978-0-615-44146-7

Library of Congress Control Number: 2011900945

Designed by Malcolm Mekaru.

For more information on the Festival of Pacific Arts: www.spc.int

For more information on the author-photographer: www.floydtakeuchi.com

Inside

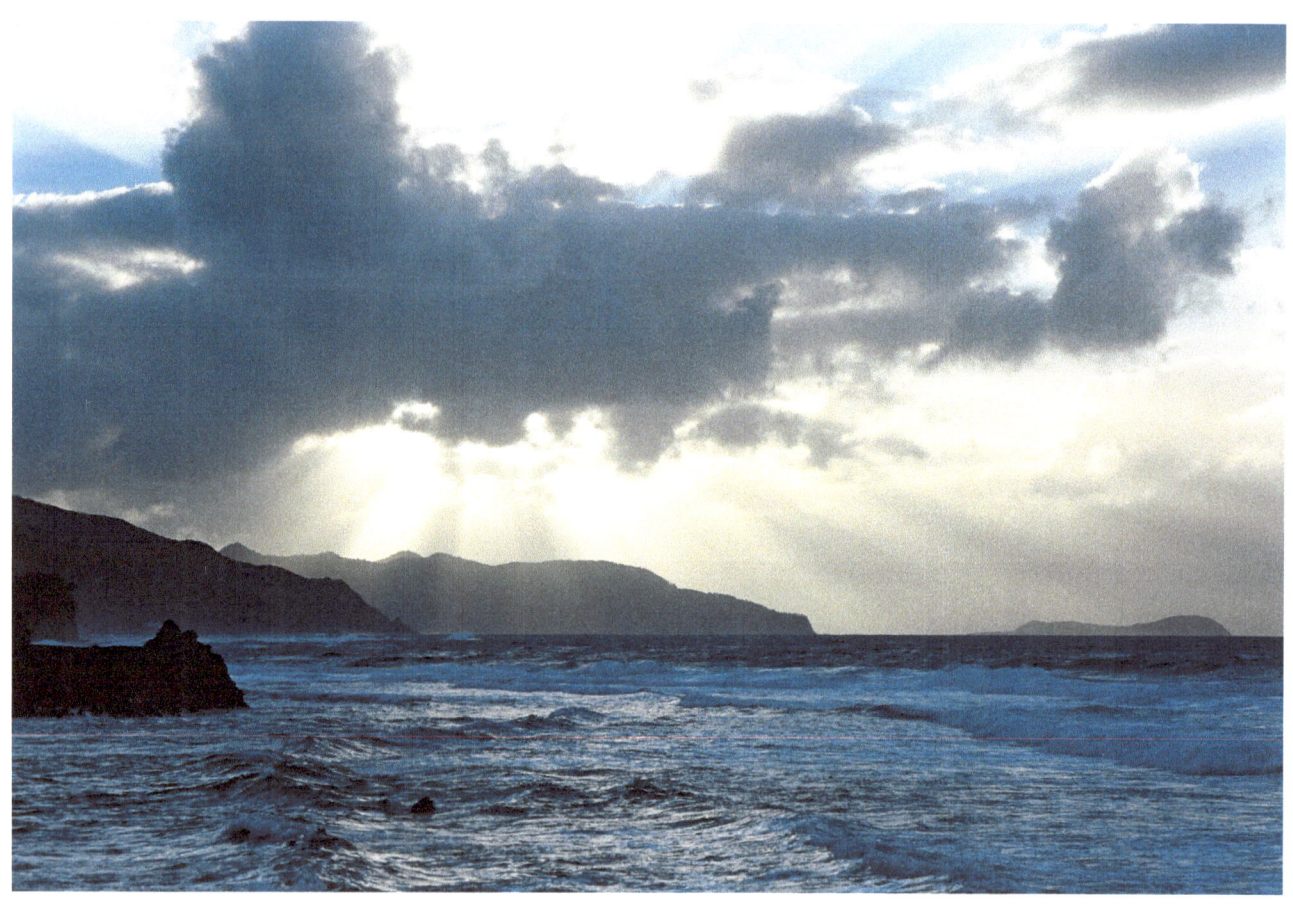

Sunrise over Tutuila, American Samoa.

Pasefika

The sky was still ink black over Pago Pago Harbor when the first bus-loads of sleepy-eyed Pacific Island dancers and performers arrived at the gymnasium. They quietly filed into the open-sided gym, directed to their proper places along the edge of the concrete-floor pavilion. The Tahitians, stunning even in the harsh gym lighting, were in white muumuus with red Polynesian print sashes around their curvy hips, some wearing hats woven from coconut fronds. The Tokelauans were in blue, the women in long skirts, the men in knee-length lava-lavas with matching shirts. The Samoans showed up in force, lined up with military precision, the women in dark blue puletasi, the men, solid, barrel-chested lads, in their lava-lavas.

The Samoana High School gymnasium in Utulei village, American Samoa was the staging area for the opening day celebrations of the 10th Festival of Pacific Arts. This gathering of Oceania's finest dancers, performers and artisans is held every four years around the Pacific, sponsored by the Secretariat of the Pacific Community. The SPC, as it is better known, is a regional organization that provides technical assistance and policy advice to member nations and territories. The first Festival was held in 1972 in Fiji. The 10th Festival, in 2008, was being held for the first time in an American insular territory.

The Festival of Pacific Arts is two amazing weeks of the best of Pacific culture, featuring the dancing, singing, carving and storytelling that makes Oceania such a draw for the rest of the world. These aren't the performances usually seen in resort hotels or on docks when cruise ships pull into Pacific ports. Rather, it is dancing at the level usually reserved for the most important traditional ceremonies in villages, performed for high-ranking chiefs and other dignitaries.

Most of the groups representing the 23 Pacific nations and territories at the Festival in American Samoa competed for the right to be at the event. They came from nations as large as Papua New Guinea, and as small as Niue. Headdresses ranged from Papua New Guinean hats woven from human hair to delicate feathers worn by the sensual dancers of Rapa Nui, or Easter Island. The islanders from Kiribati, in the Central Pacific, brought their thick grass skirts and intricately woven jewelry made from coconut and pandanus leaves. The Tongans wrapped themselves in stunning tapa, their distinctive print designs framing beautiful mocha-colored skin dripping with coconut oil. There was even a young woman from Norfolk Island, their only dancer, a delicate beauty whose people trace their lineage from the British sailors who mutinied aboard the HMS Bounty, and the Tahitians who traveled with them.

The islanders came from all corners of the Pacific – most from Polynesia, whose islands such as Tahiti and Samoa are the stuff of legend. The three corners of Polynesia were represented: Hawaii to the north, Rapa Nui or Easter Island to the east, and New Zealand, Aotearoa as its indigenous Maori call their islands, to the south. The dark-skinned Melanesians were there, too, most from Papua New Guinea, which has some six million of Oceania's seven million-plus inhabitants. But the Solomon Islands, home to dancers who perform panpipes, were also there, along with a stunning troupe from the French territory of New Caledonia. Dancers representing Micronesia, islands in the Central and Western Pacific, came from Kiribati, Palau and Guam.

On the 10th Festival's opening day, as light began to gather in the tropical sky, the Samoana High School Gymnasium was full. Delegations were in their proper places, waiting for the signal to line up on the road that fronts the building, and then march along the Pago Pago Harbor waterfront to the great malae, or meeting area, before American Samoa's Fono, or legislature. But Pacific Islanders being Pacific Islanders, they weren't going to be content to stare at the gym's ceiling. The first sounds of restless energy came, not surprisingly, from the Cook Islanders. It was the sound of their wood slit drum, an insistent rat-tat-tat beat that caused heads to turn. Quickly, Cook Islands dancers wearing yellow T-shirts jumped up and began their hip-swinging, energetic dancing. It was just past 6 a.m., and this group clearly didn't need coffee to get its day going.

And performers being performers, the other delegations weren't going to let the Cook Islanders steal the show. Soon, a number of Tahitian men and women joined their Cook Island cousins, smiles as wide as billboards, feet moving quickly, hips a blur as they moved to the fast beat. The battle of the dancers was joined, with the Tahitians trying to outdo the Cook Islanders, and the Cooks responding in kind.

But then the Tokelauans, strikingly beautiful Polynesians from a New Zealand protectorate near Samoa, joined the fray. They lined up, men and women, and the fast beat of their music began to fill the gymnasium, too. They were not going to let the rest of the huge crowd think the Tahitians and Cook Islanders were the only Polynesians who could put on a show.

Not to be outdone, the Rapa Nui delegation rose to its feet. This delegation was a physical group, the men dancing with strong, warrior-like thrusts of their arms and hips, the women more graceful, but still dancing with sinuous moves. While they speak Spanish, Rapa Nui being part of Chile, these Polynesians know how to communicate with their dancing. Their physical, sensual dancing, in front of the conservative Samoans, was a visual study in the diversity of Polynesian cultures. Perhaps no difference was more evident than in the Rapa Nui costumes, mostly body paint and feathers, compared with the Samoan puletasi, a long skirt with a matching form-fitting tunic. The pueltasi accentuates female curves, and some designs can be downright suggestive, but even a tight puletasi is more modest than white paint on exposed buttocks.

Thus the tone was set for the next two weeks – good-natured competition, sharing and comparing, mutual admiration societies formed at the many performance venues on Tutuila, American Samoa's main island.

The Festival of Pacific Arts may be the pinnacle of Oceanic cultural events, but being able to enjoy the event can be a challenge for even an intrepid visitor. The 10th Festival in American Samoa was a good example: with usually only two flights a week to Pago Pago from Hawaii and about 200 hotel rooms in the territory, being able to get to the program, let alone find a place to stay during the two-week event, was a challenge. Nearly all of the 2,000-plus national delegates who took part in the 10th Festival were housed in public schools converted into makeshift dormitories.

But it is worth the planning and effort to attend a Festival of Pacific Arts, no matter how challenging the exercise. The Festival is a blur of color and culture, and the ability to walk among performers, chat with them, and make new friends is unmatched by any other cultural event in the Pacific. It is a chance to see the core strength of Oceania: cultures based on generations of learning to do much with relatively little; beauty shaped by eons of living in some of the most beautiful places on Earth; unabashed joy in sharing ancient and modern traditions of song and dance.

Even for those of us who have traveled around the region, there was much to learn. For example, I had worked in Fiji, but never had the chance to sit before islanders from Rotuma, a Polynesian outpost in Melanesian Fiji, as they sang and danced with their hypnotic harmony. At the Festival, the Rotumans became one of my favorite groups to watch, again and again. I've been to Kiribati, briefly, and had seen their dancers perform in the past. But the group at the Festival of Pacific Arts, chosen in a national competition, the lead dancer told me proudly, was stunning. There were few groups that displayed such joy and energy on stage, or that offered such a warm welcome off-stage.

The sweet smell of coconut oil mixed with sweat and the fragrance of tropical flowers became the perfume of the pageant. It blended with visuals that could be overwhelming – a Tokelauan beauty queen wearing a shell headdress walking past a confident Rapa Nui dancer dressed only in a loincloth and body paint; bare-breasted Papua New Guinea female dancers with feathers in their hair chatting with young Samoan performers wearing brightly-colored puletasi and lava-lavas; an Australian aborigine dancer, in dramatic body paint, sitting with an American Samoan guide in the shade of a fale, both reading from a Festival booklet.

Performances were held under the blazing tropical sun on a stage next to Pago Pago Harbor, one of the most beautiful anchorages in the Pacific Islands. Dancers also performed at the stage on the Fagatogo village malae, usually the venue for major Samoan celebrations. A number of large evening performances were held at American Samoa's sports stadium in Tafuna village, near the territory's airport. There, someone had the idea that a rainbow of lights during evening performances was a great way to showcase brightly colored costumes. The result was something akin to putting a large village ceremony in a 1970s disco.

But if there were the occasional rough edges to some aspects of the Festival, in the end they were all part of the event's unique Pacific charm. It was a reminder that the Festival of Pacific Arts isn't Disney World; it is the real thing.

American Samoan chief and police officers greet participants during the 10th Festival of Pacific Arts' opening parade.

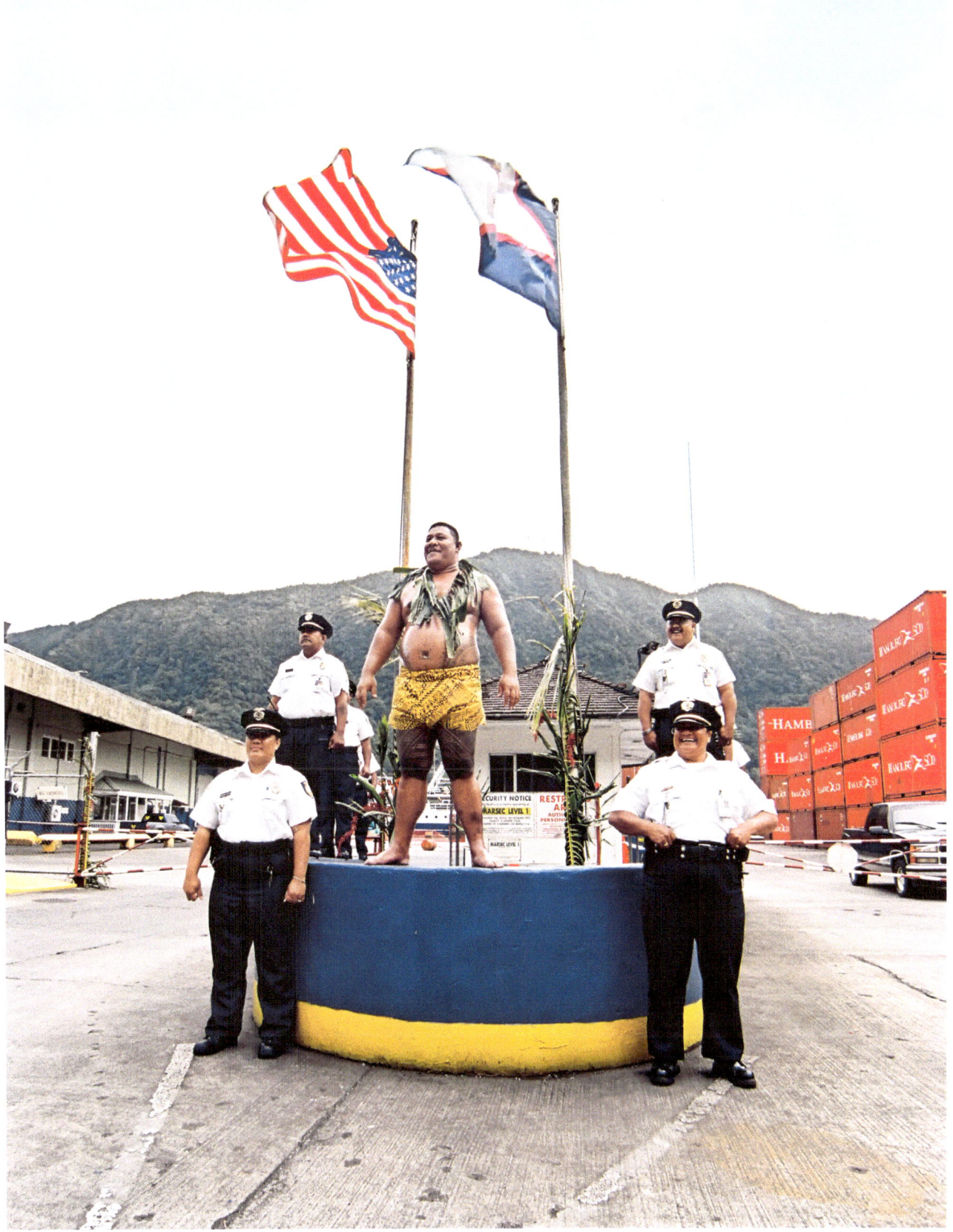

An American Samoan choir from the Kanana Fou Theological Seminary during the service to mark the opening of the 10th Festival of Pacific Arts.

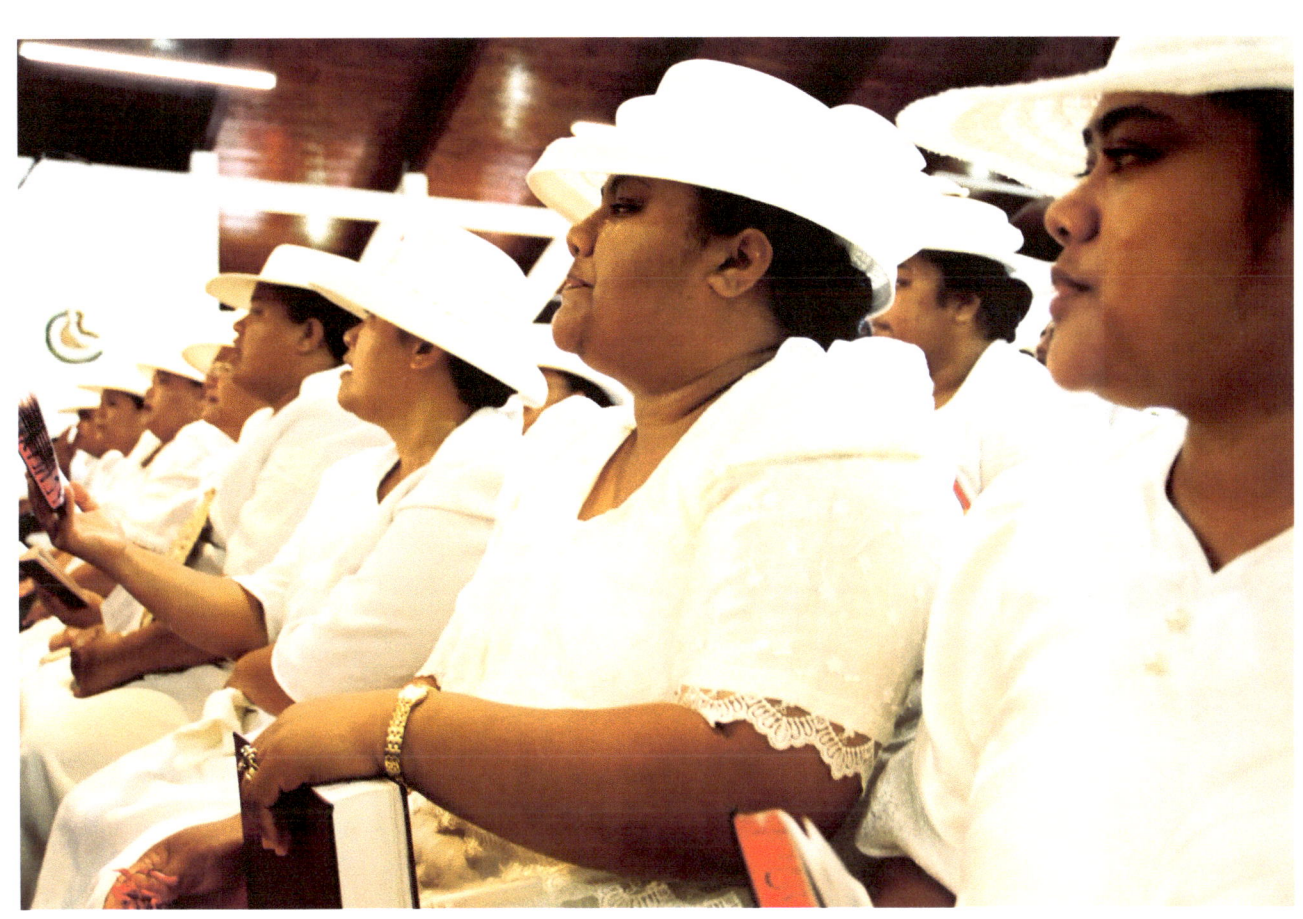

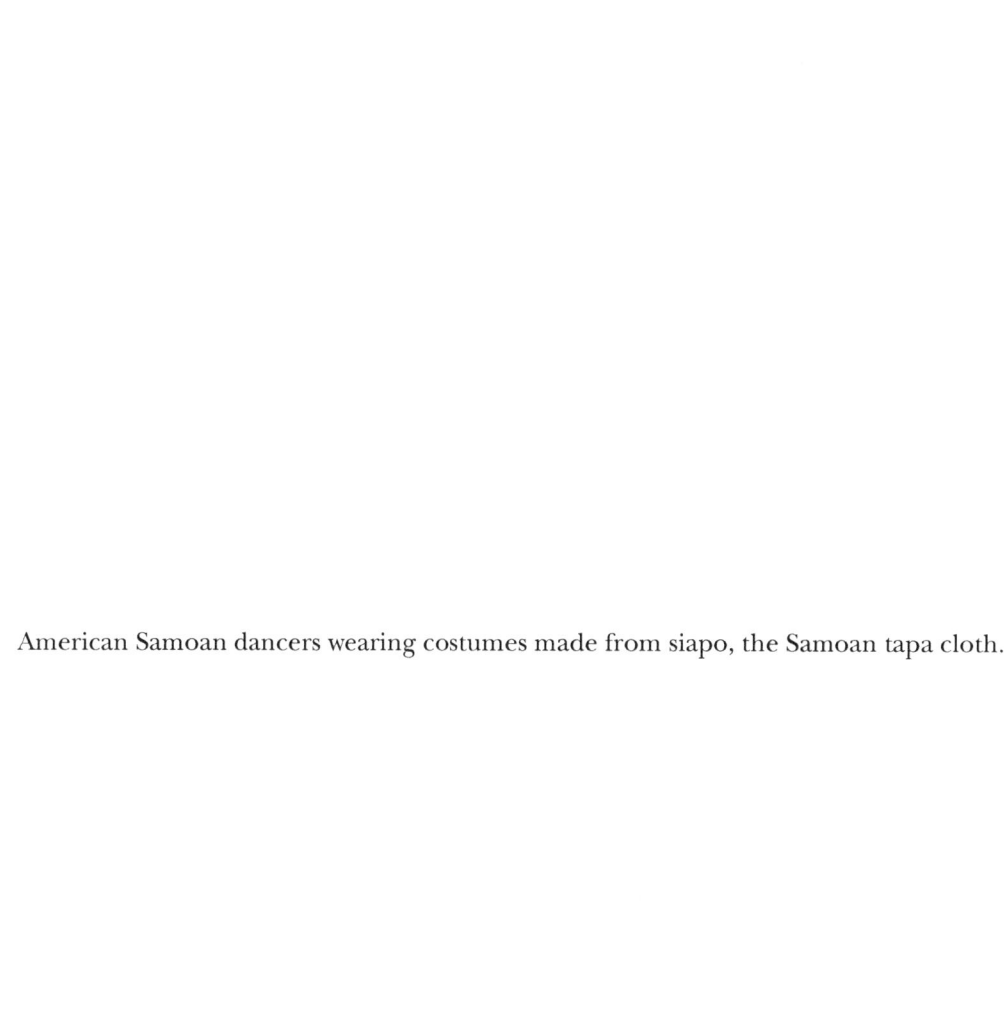

American Samoan dancers wearing costumes made from siapo, the Samoan tapa cloth.

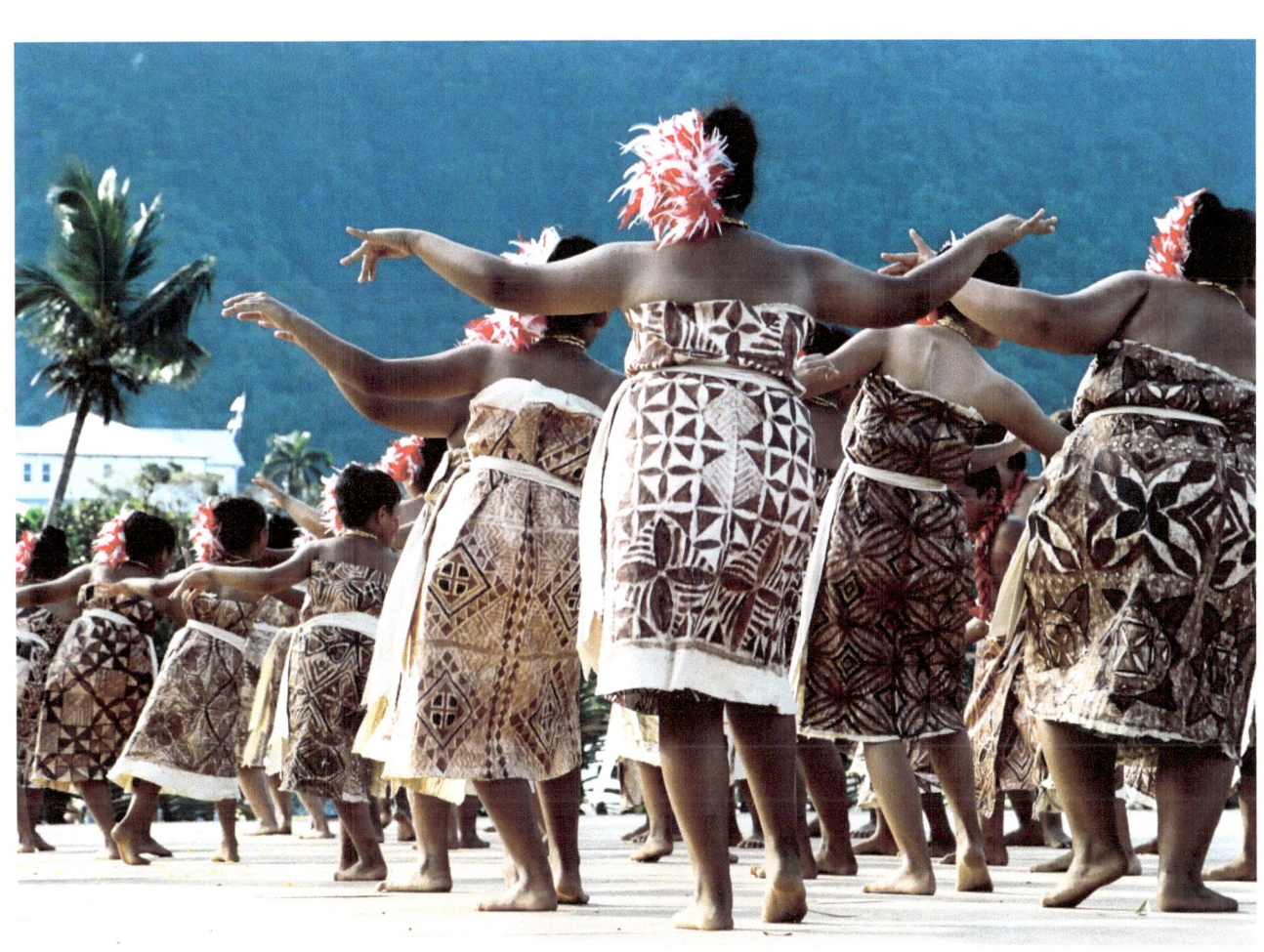

American Samoan dancers.

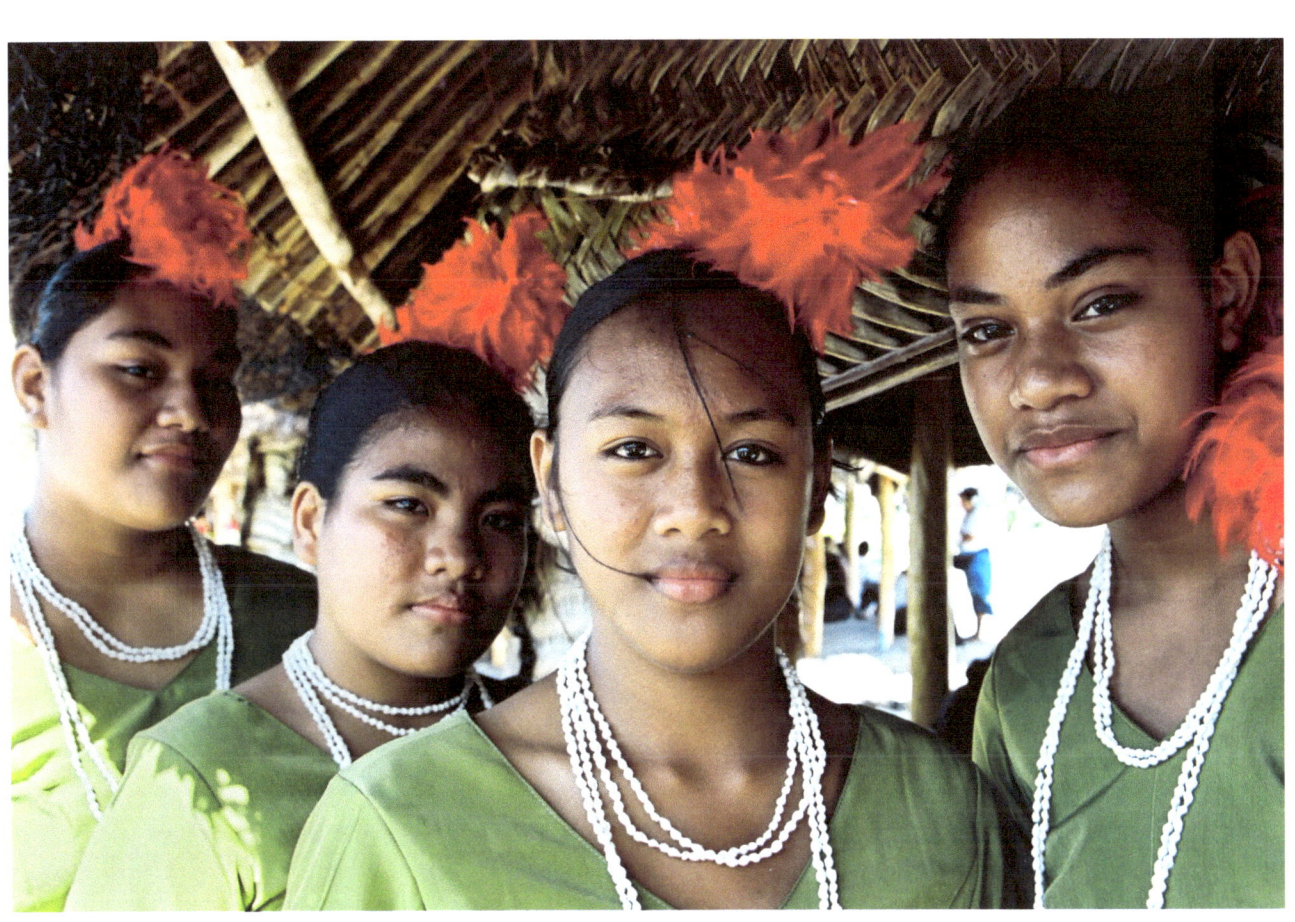

American Samoan dancers watch another group perform on the Utulei Beach stage.

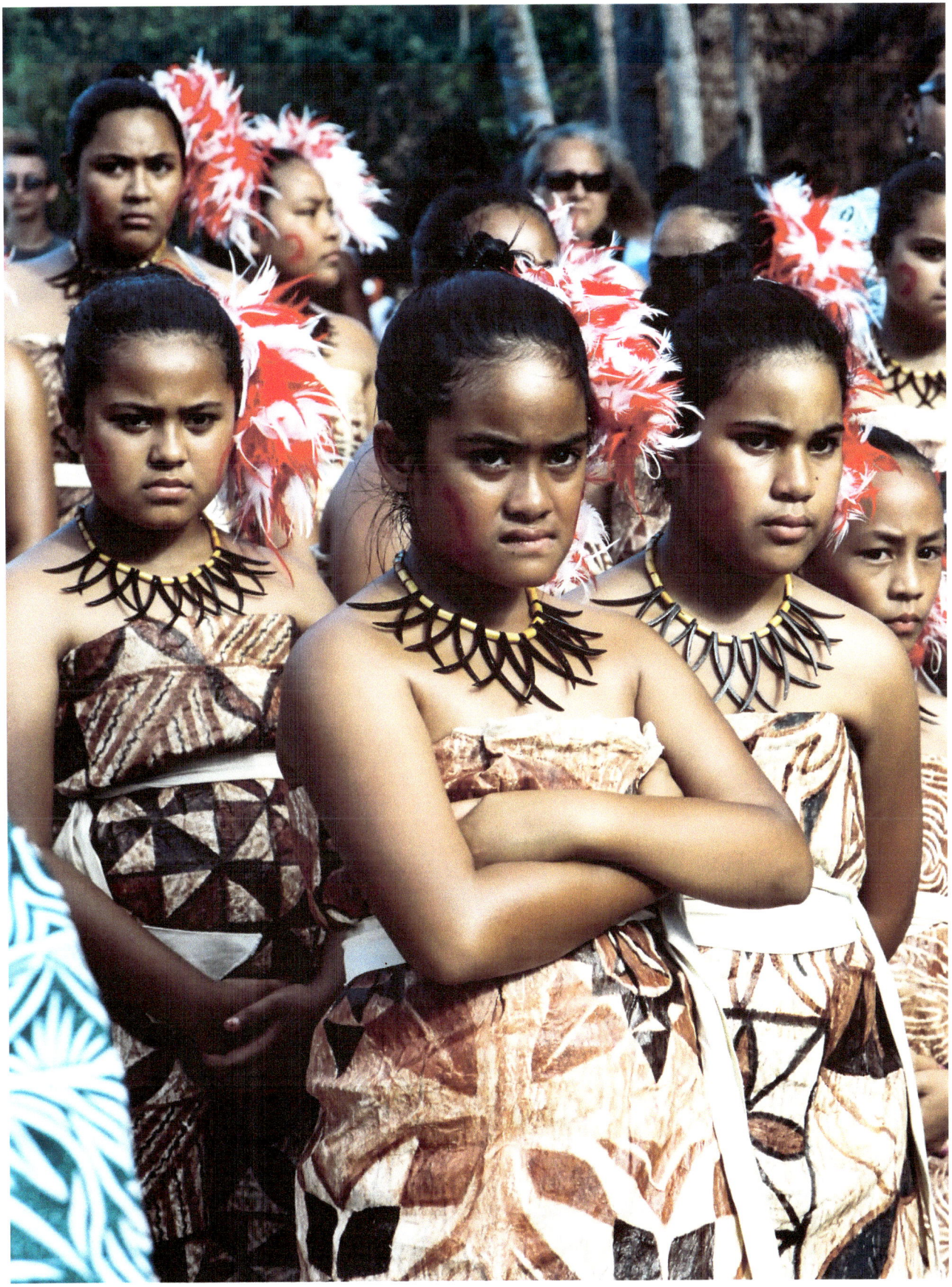

An American Samoan dancer portrays the taupou, traditionally the daughter of a high chief. She is dancing the taualunga.

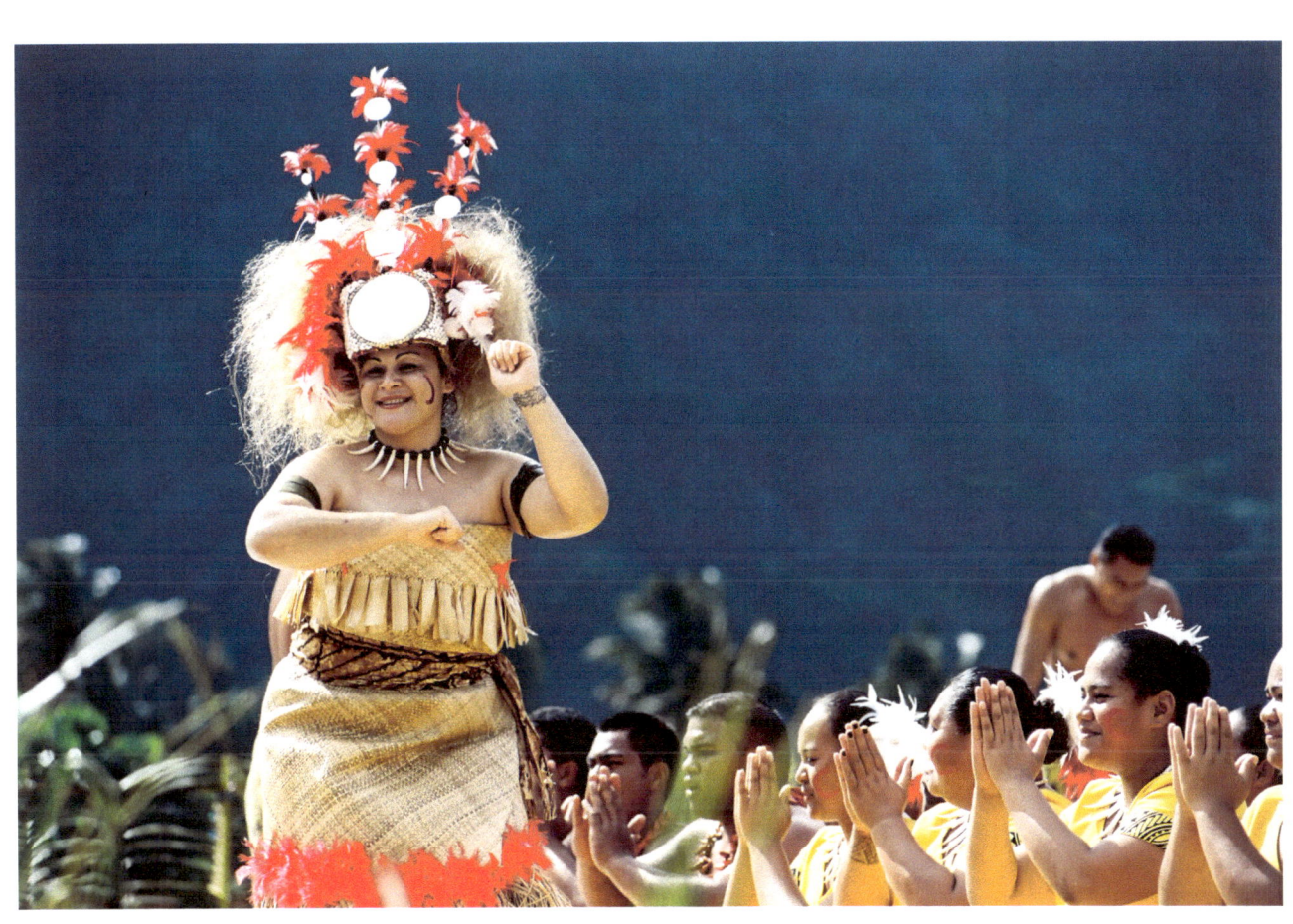

American Samoans with their malu, or tattoos, which are worn exclusively by women. Young women usually get a malu when they are teen-agers.

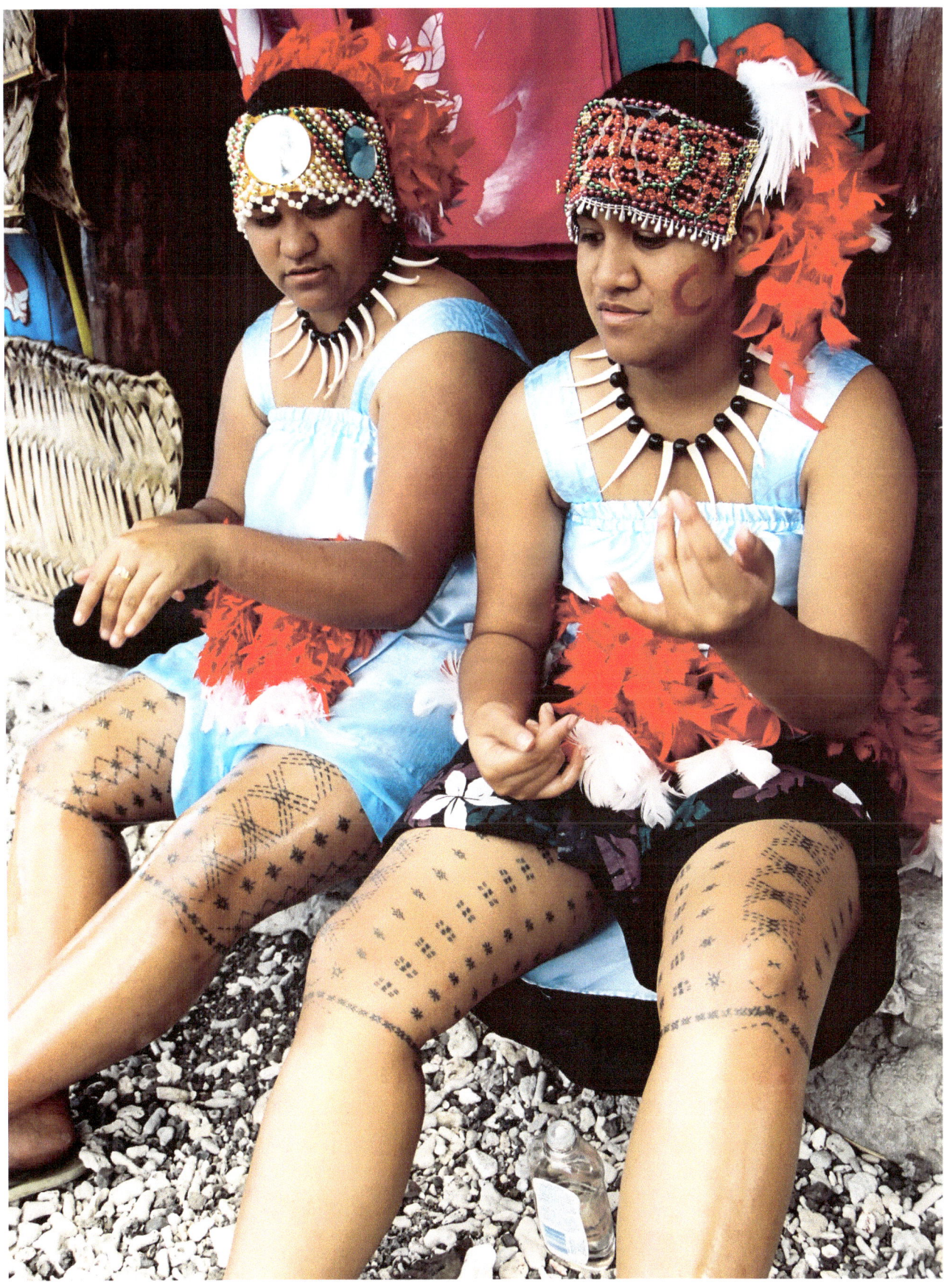

American Samoa dancers perform on the stage at the national stadium in Tafuna village.

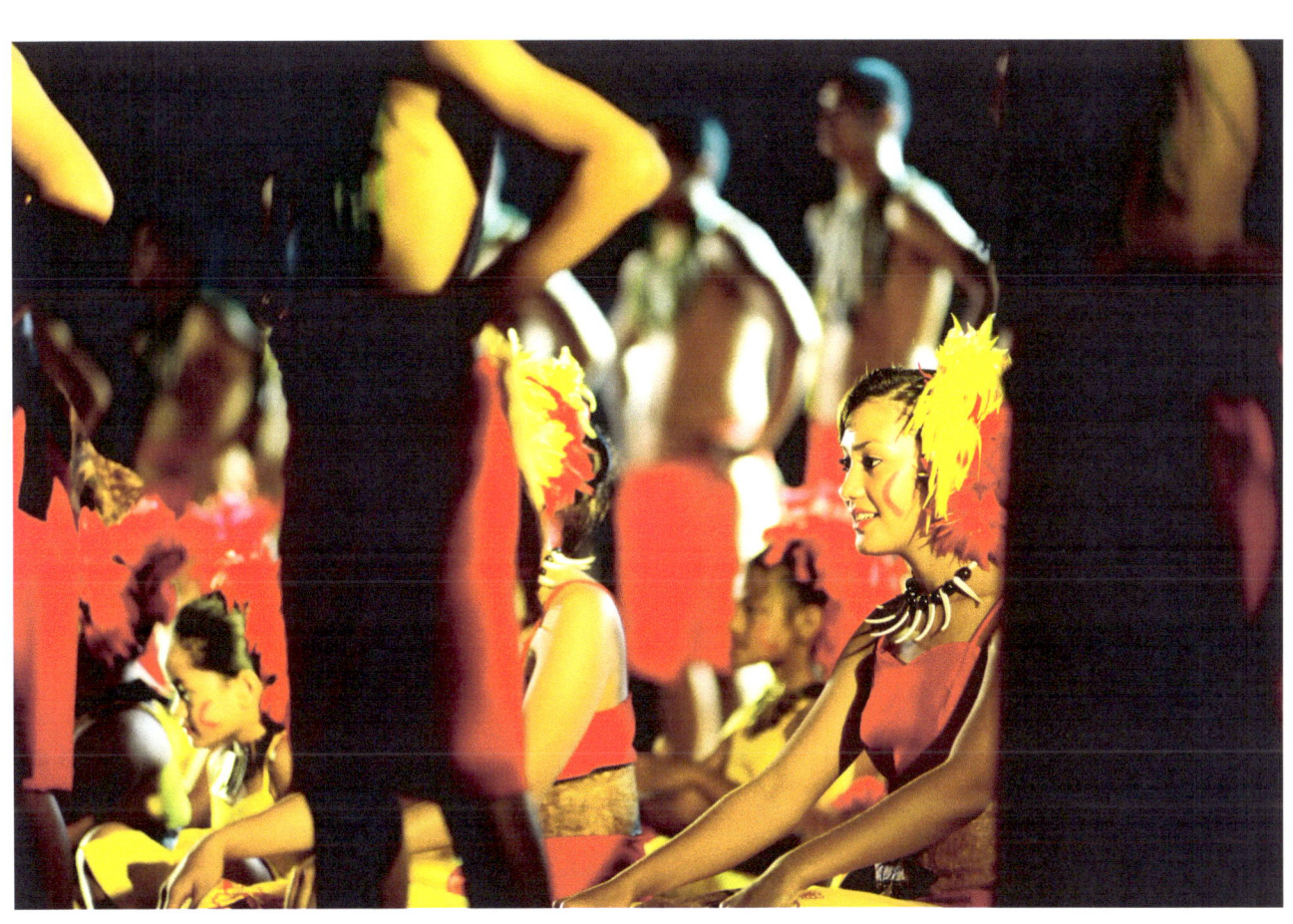

An American Samoan dancer who is part of a performing group from San Diego, California.

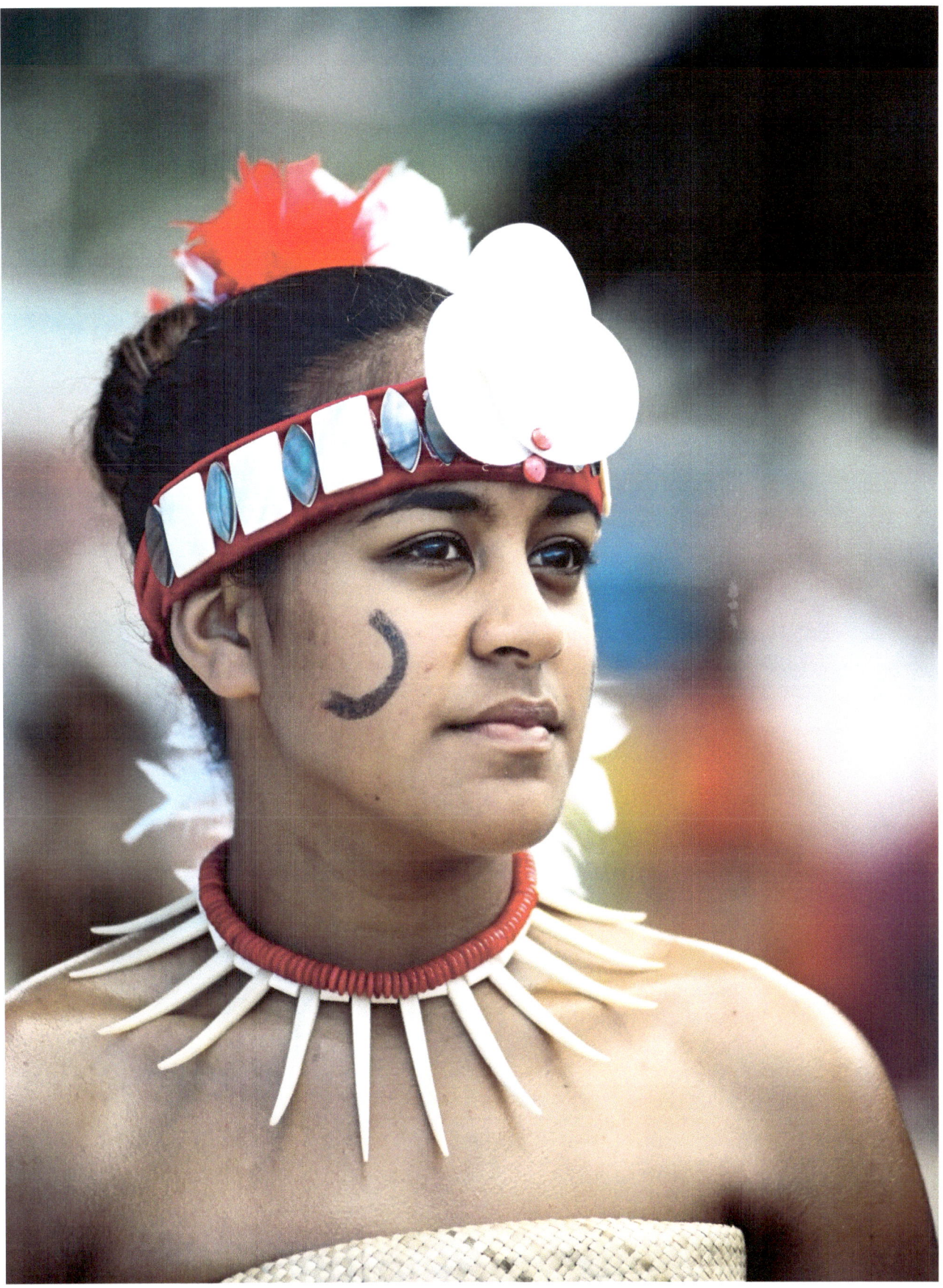

An American Samoan taupou, part of a troupe from San Diego, California, prepares kava during a performance.

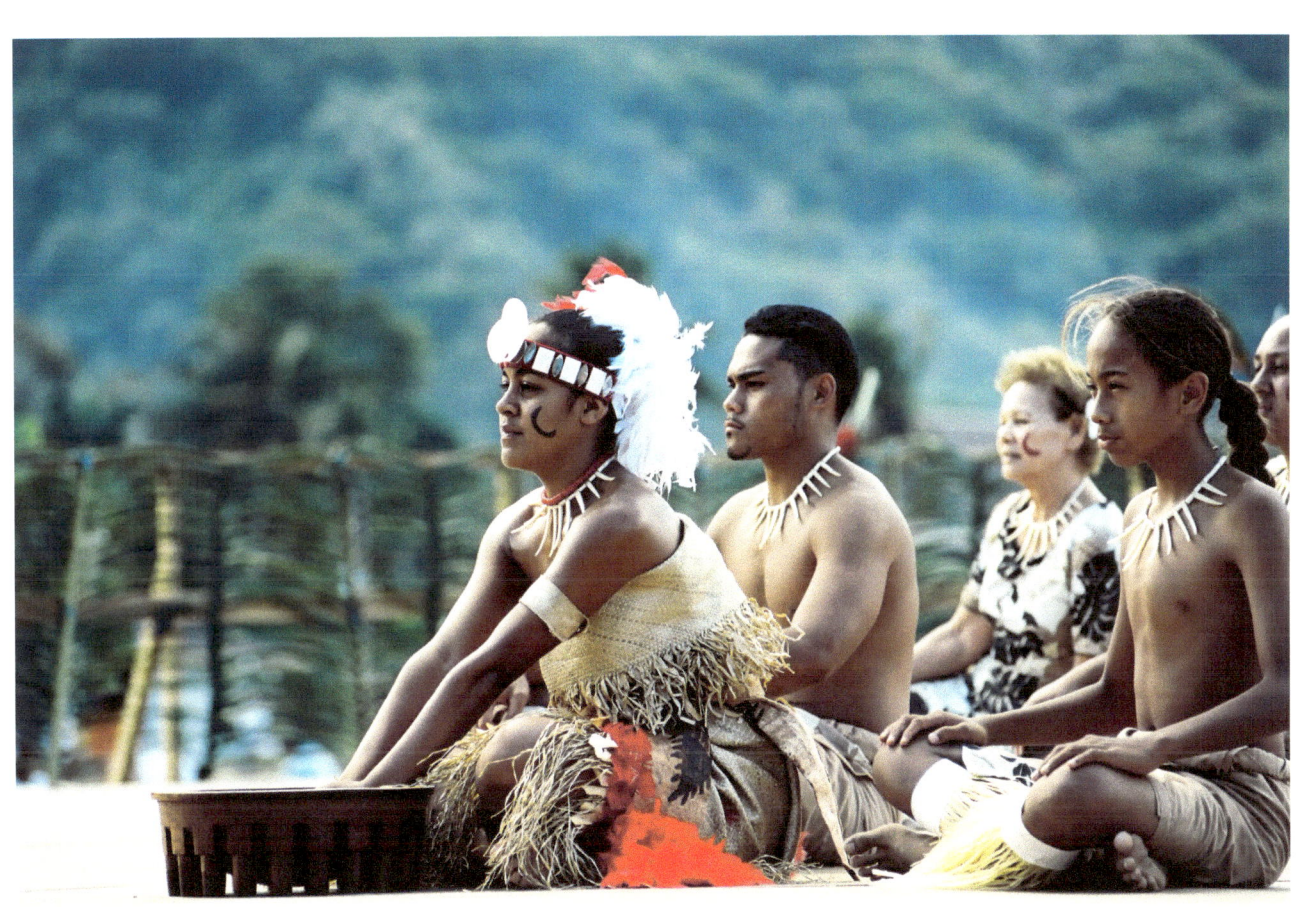

A member of the Australian aborigine group reads the Festival of Pacific Arts guide with a liaison from American Samoa.

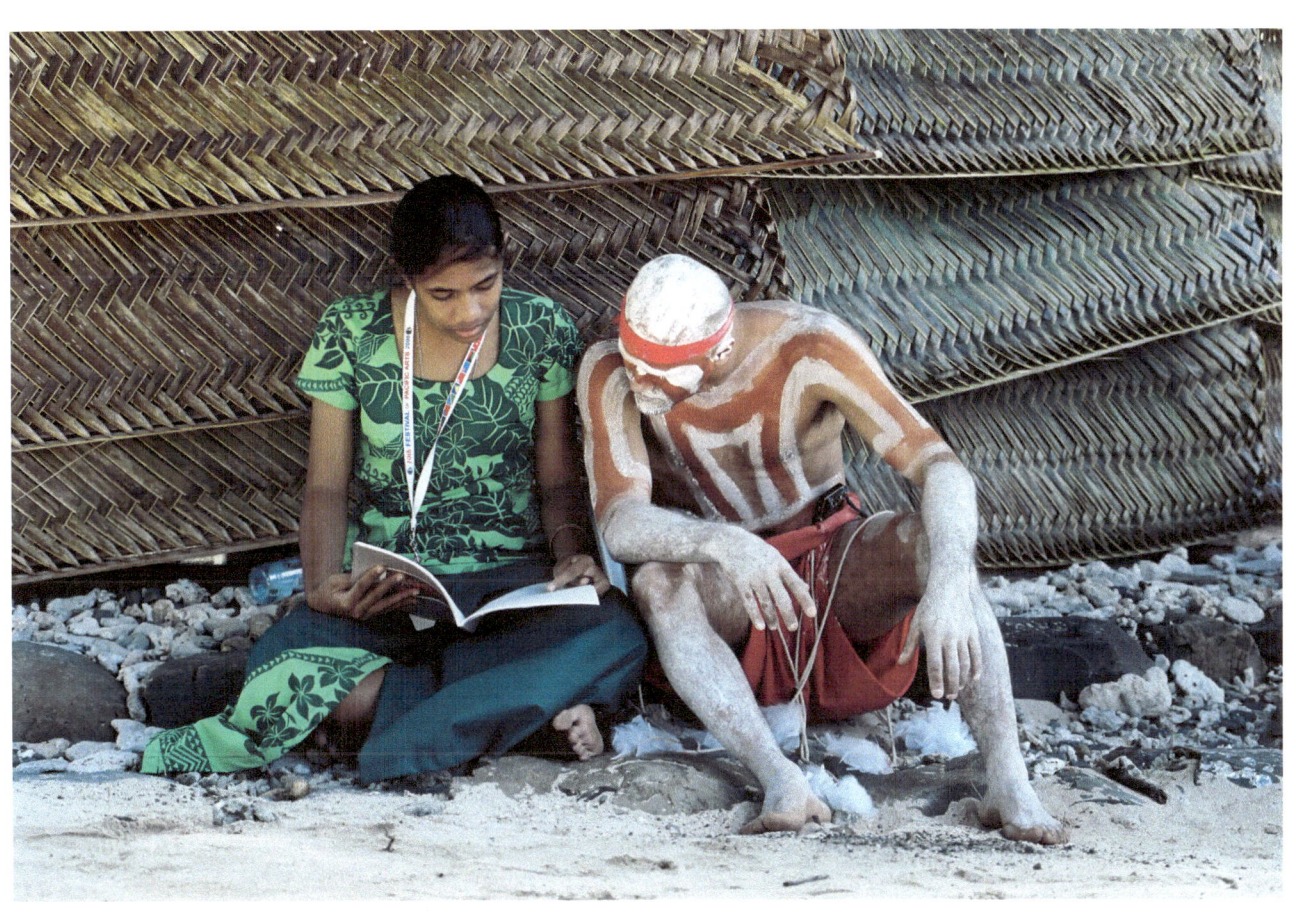

Two Australian aborigines make traditional animal skin wraps, which were later worn during the Festival's fashion shows.

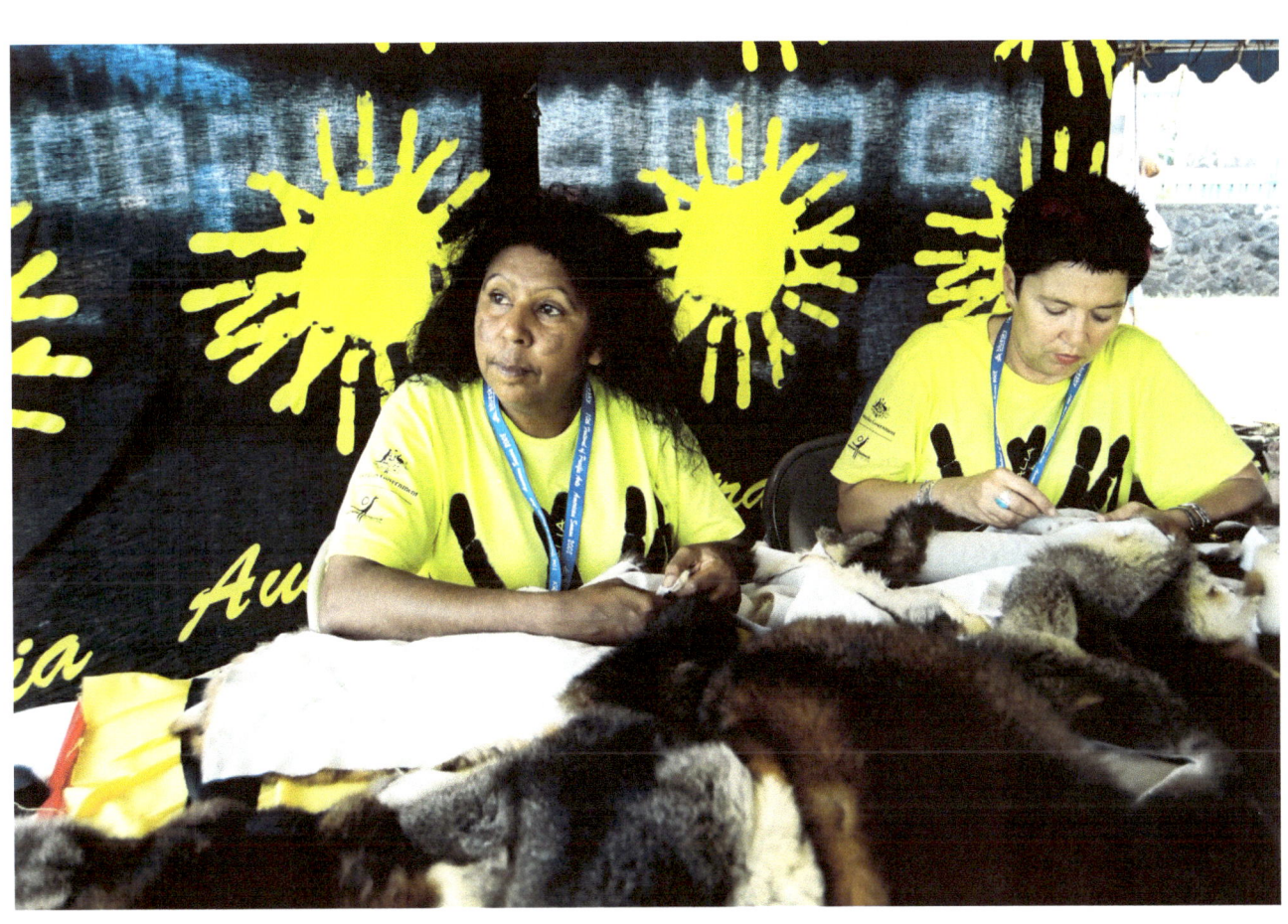

Cook Islanders put on an impromptu performance as national delegations gathered before sunrise at the Samoana High School gym on the Festival's opening day.

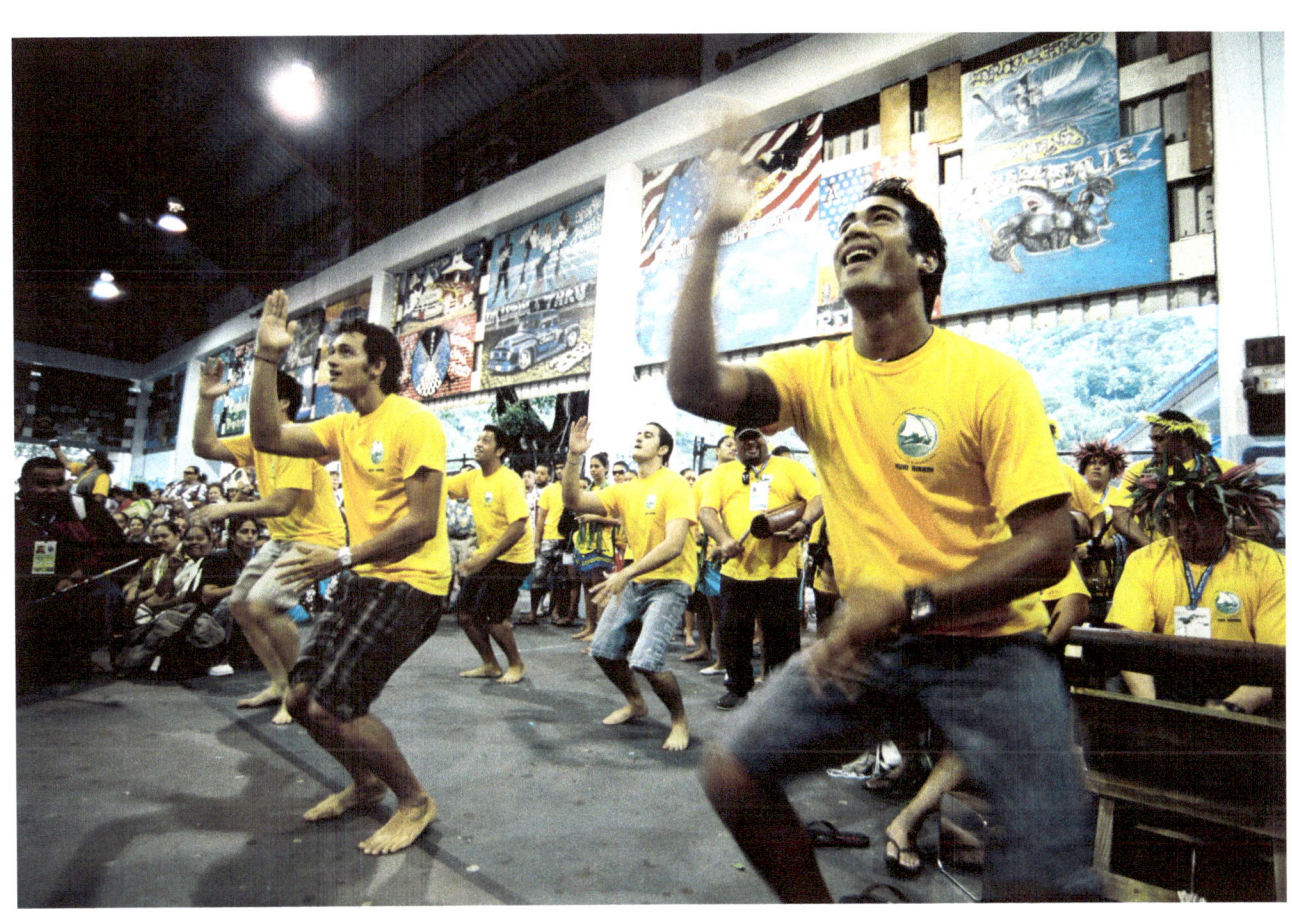

Dancers from the Cook Islands.

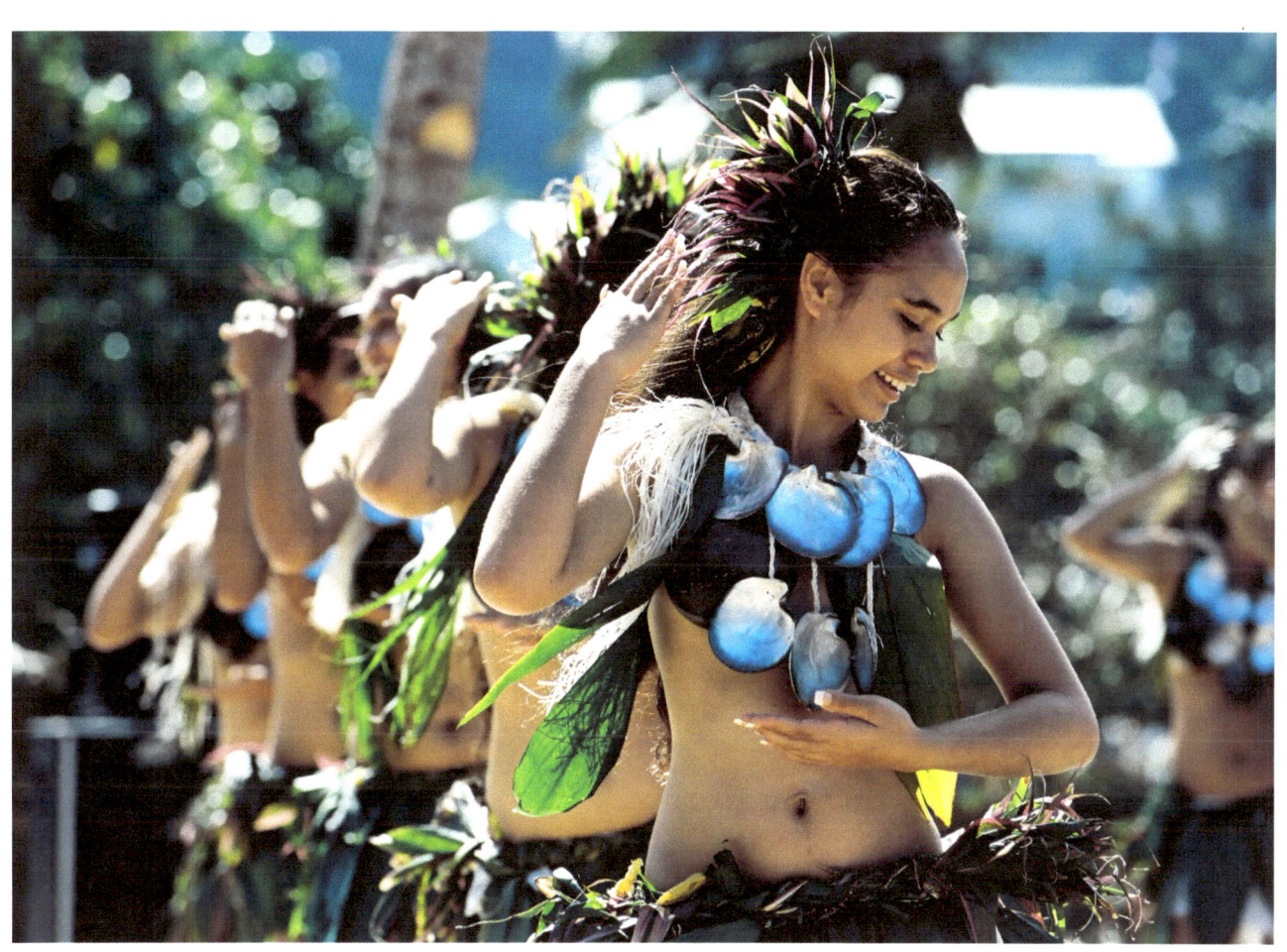

Dancers from the Cook Islanders.

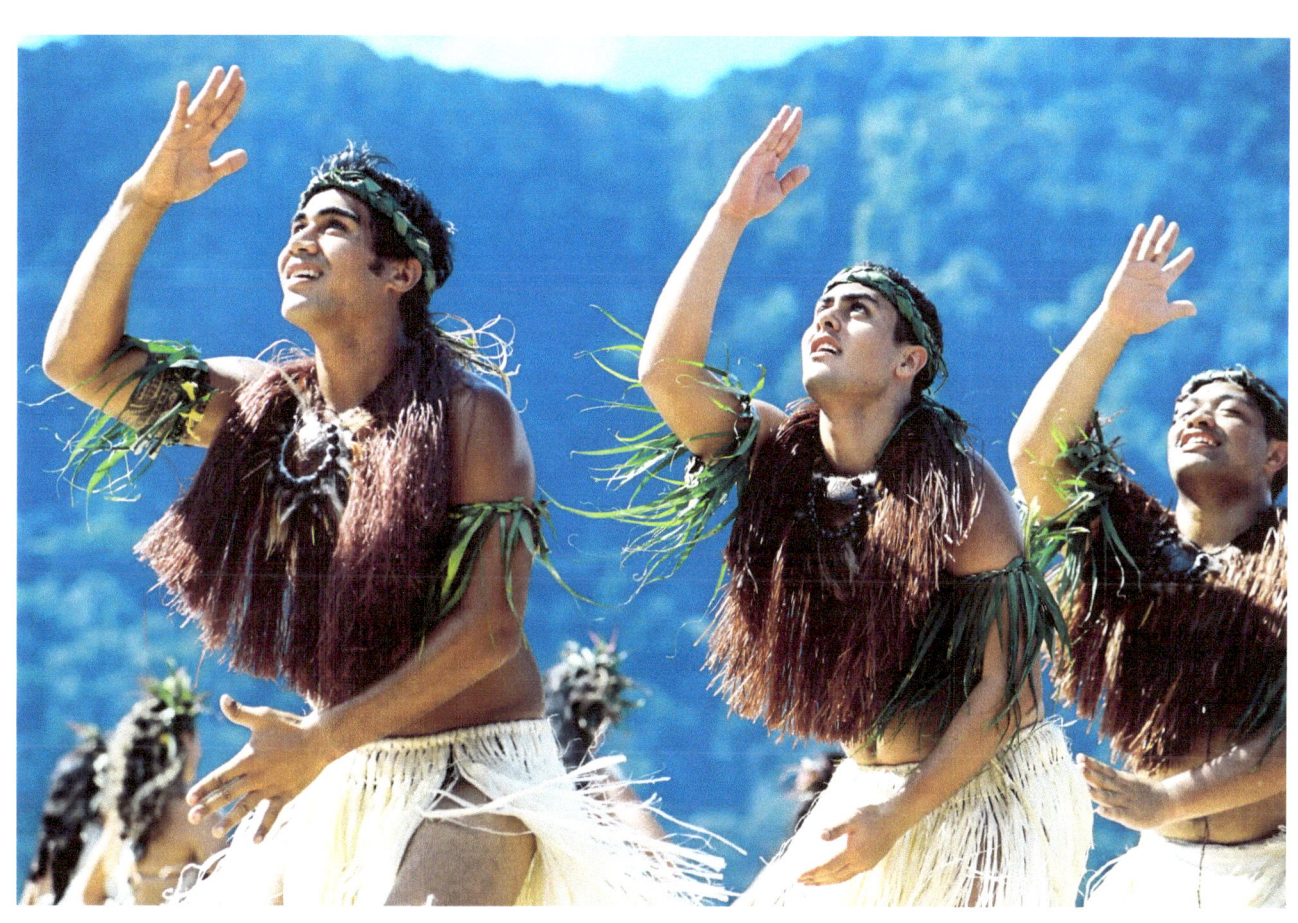

A member of Fiji's contemporary dance troupe.

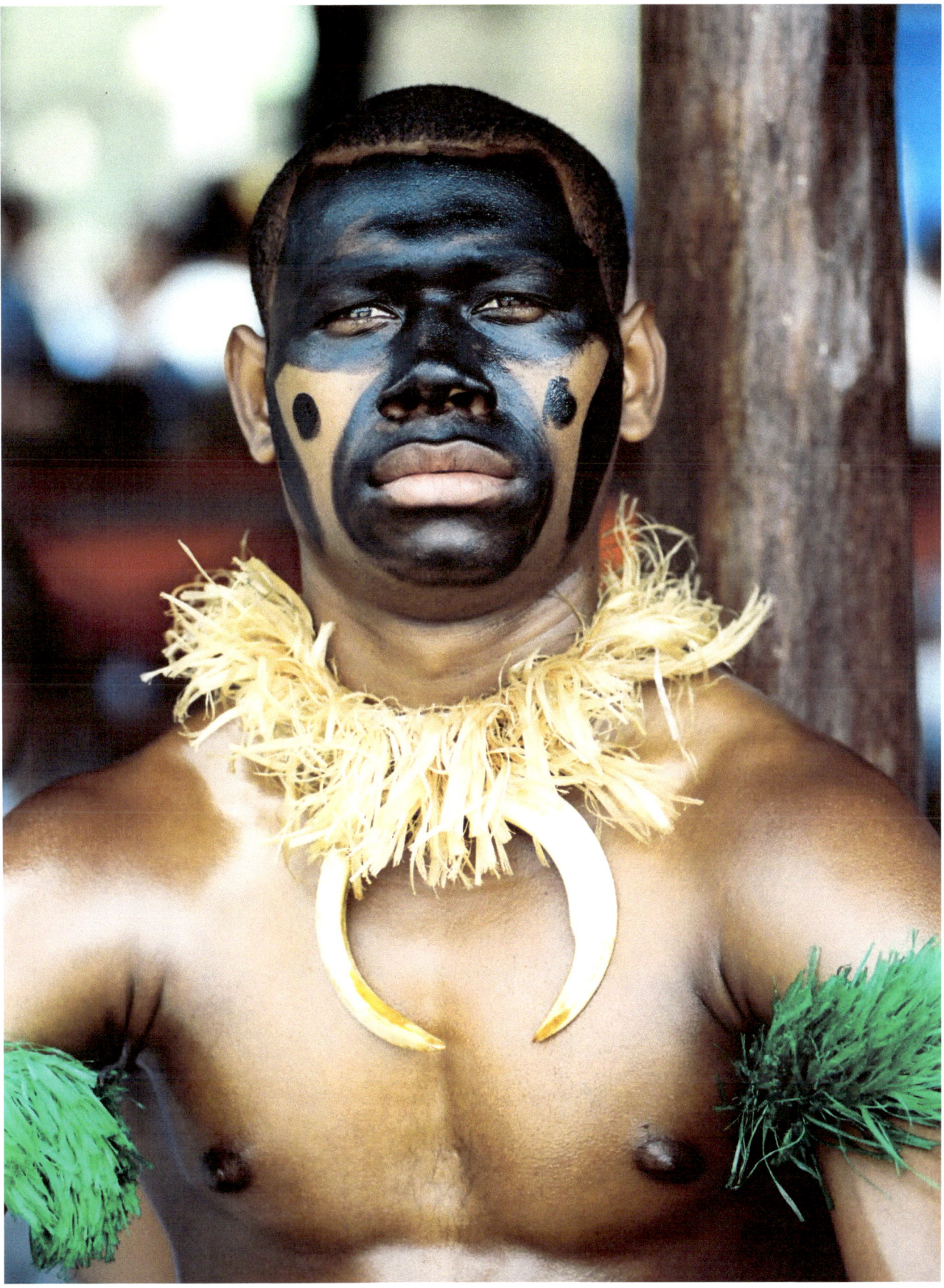

Fijian dancers perform a traditional dance using spears.

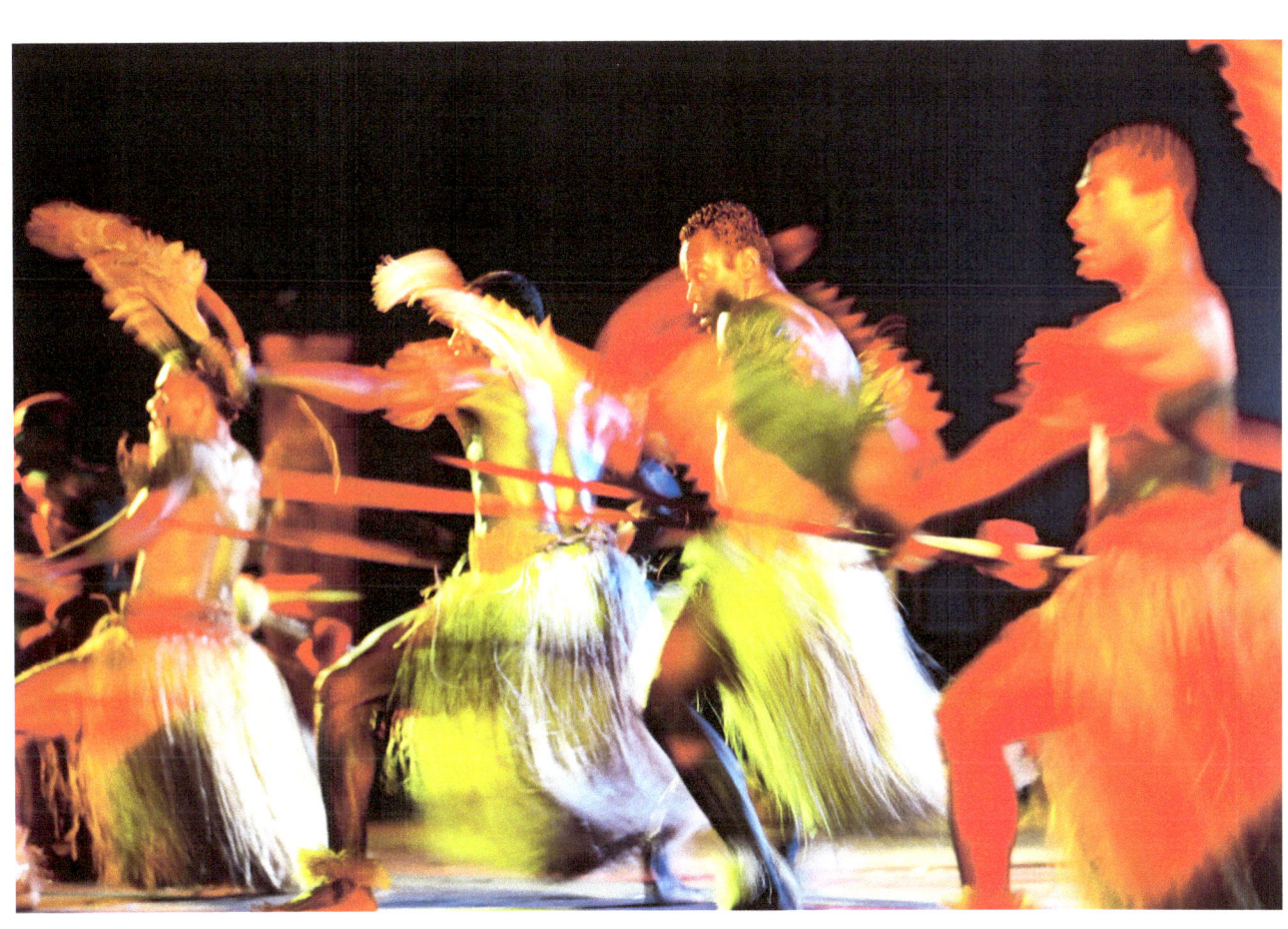

Fijians living in American Samoa hosted a private party in Tafuna village for members of the large Fiji delegation. The performers thanked their hosts by putting on a performance.

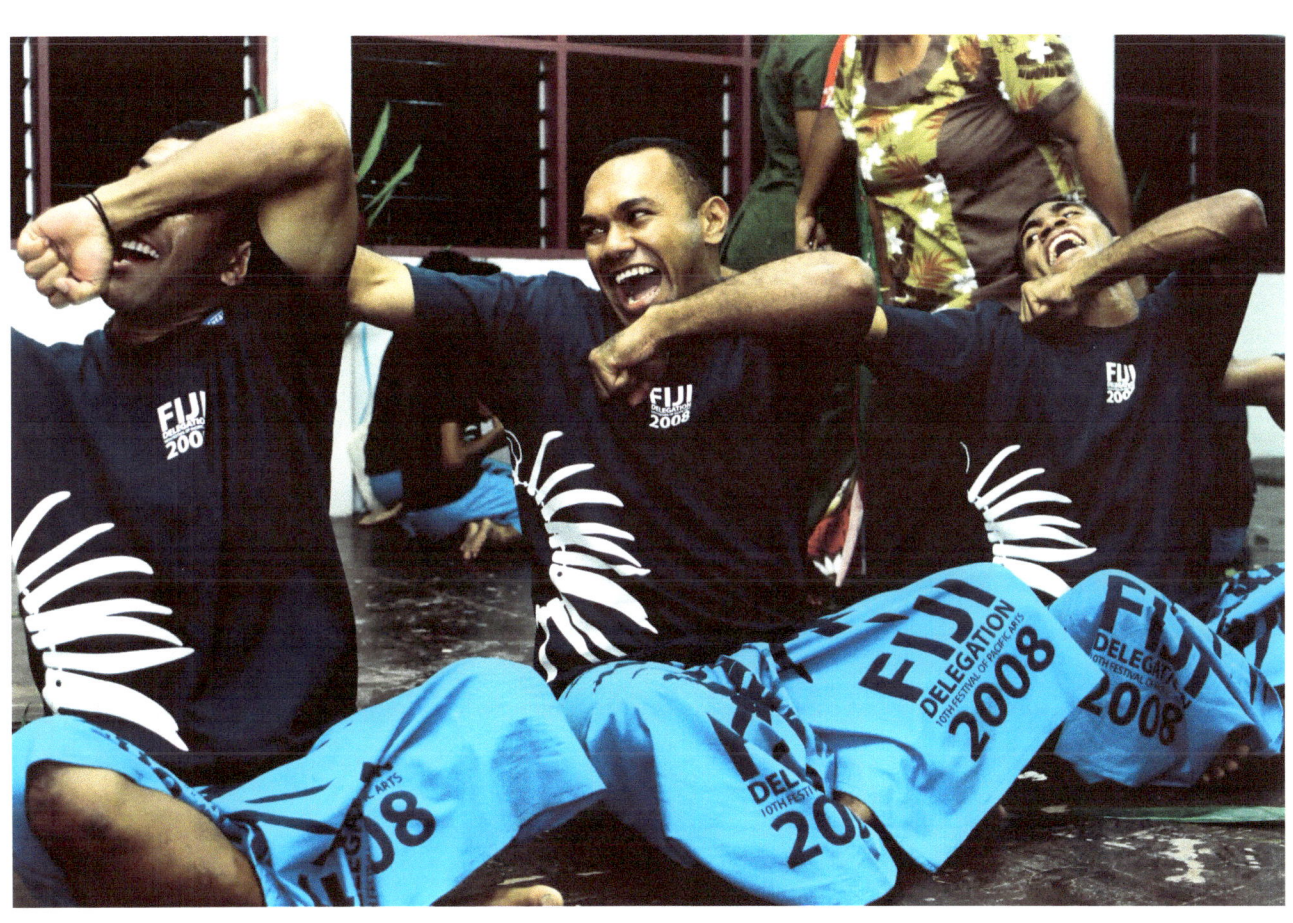

This performer was a part of the Fiji delegation's modern dance troupe.

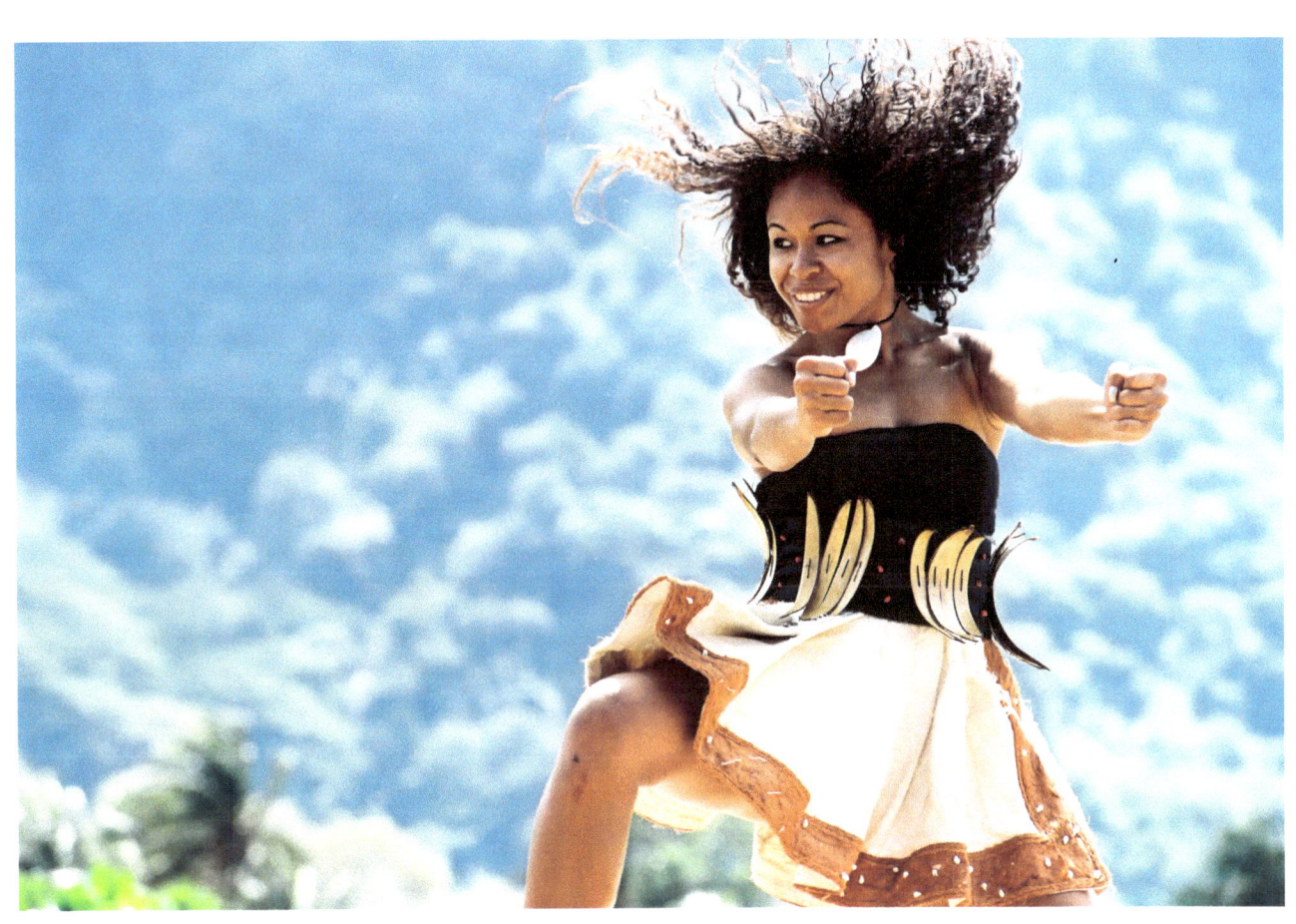

Dancers from Rotuma, a Polynesian island that is part of Fiji, perform during the welcome party for the delegation by Fijians in American Samoa.

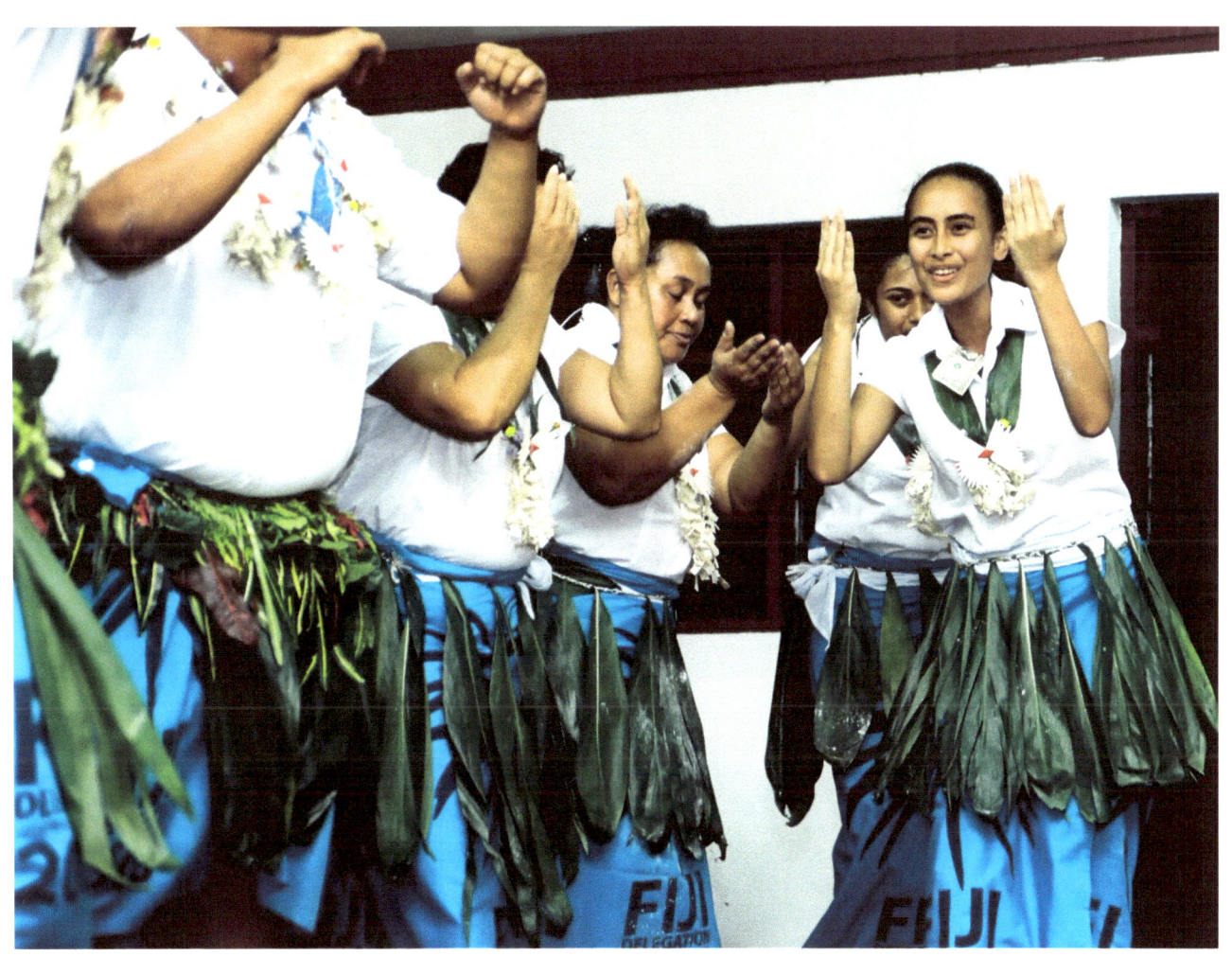

Members of the Rotuma dance group, part of the Fiji delegation.

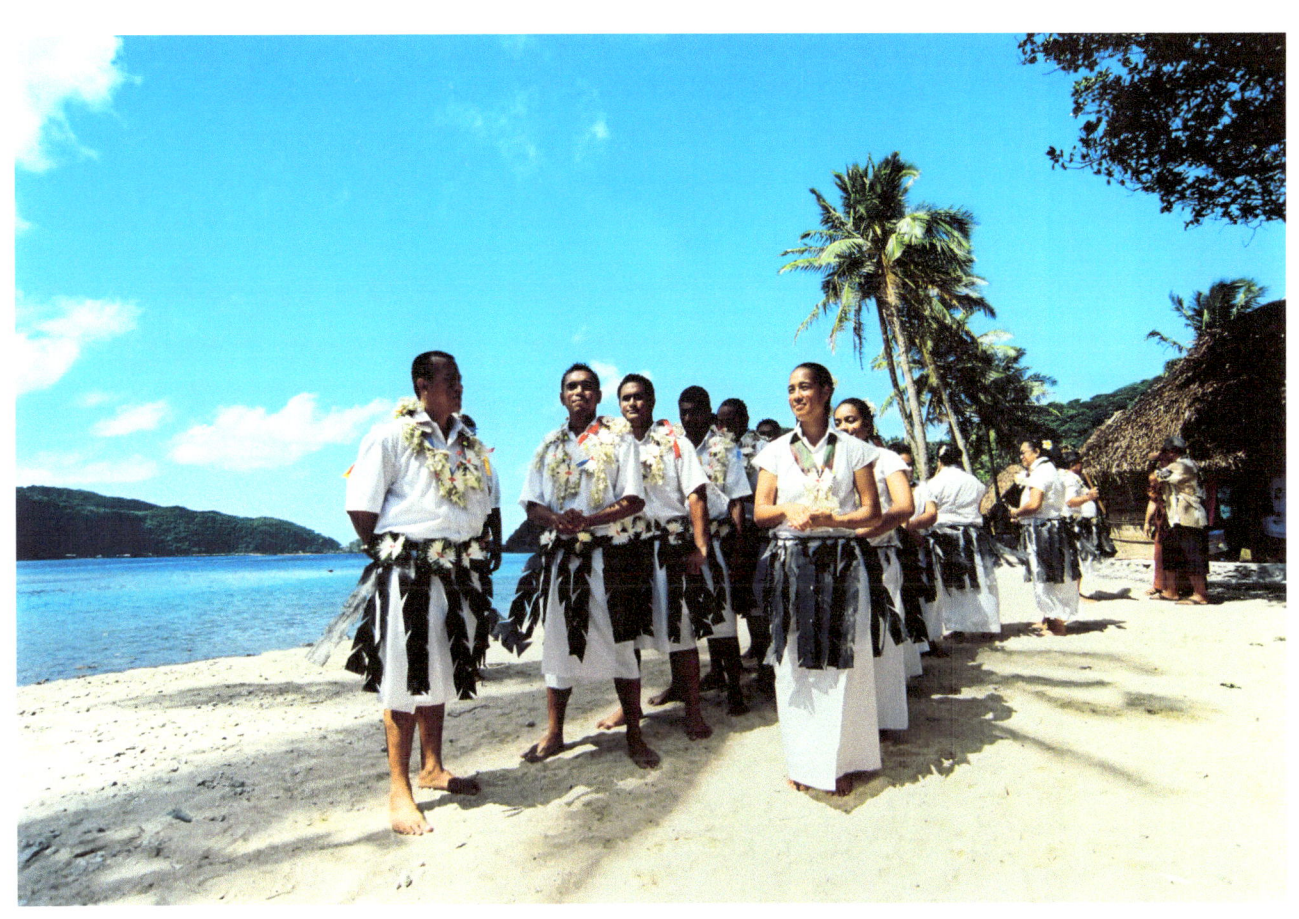

Dancers from Guam.

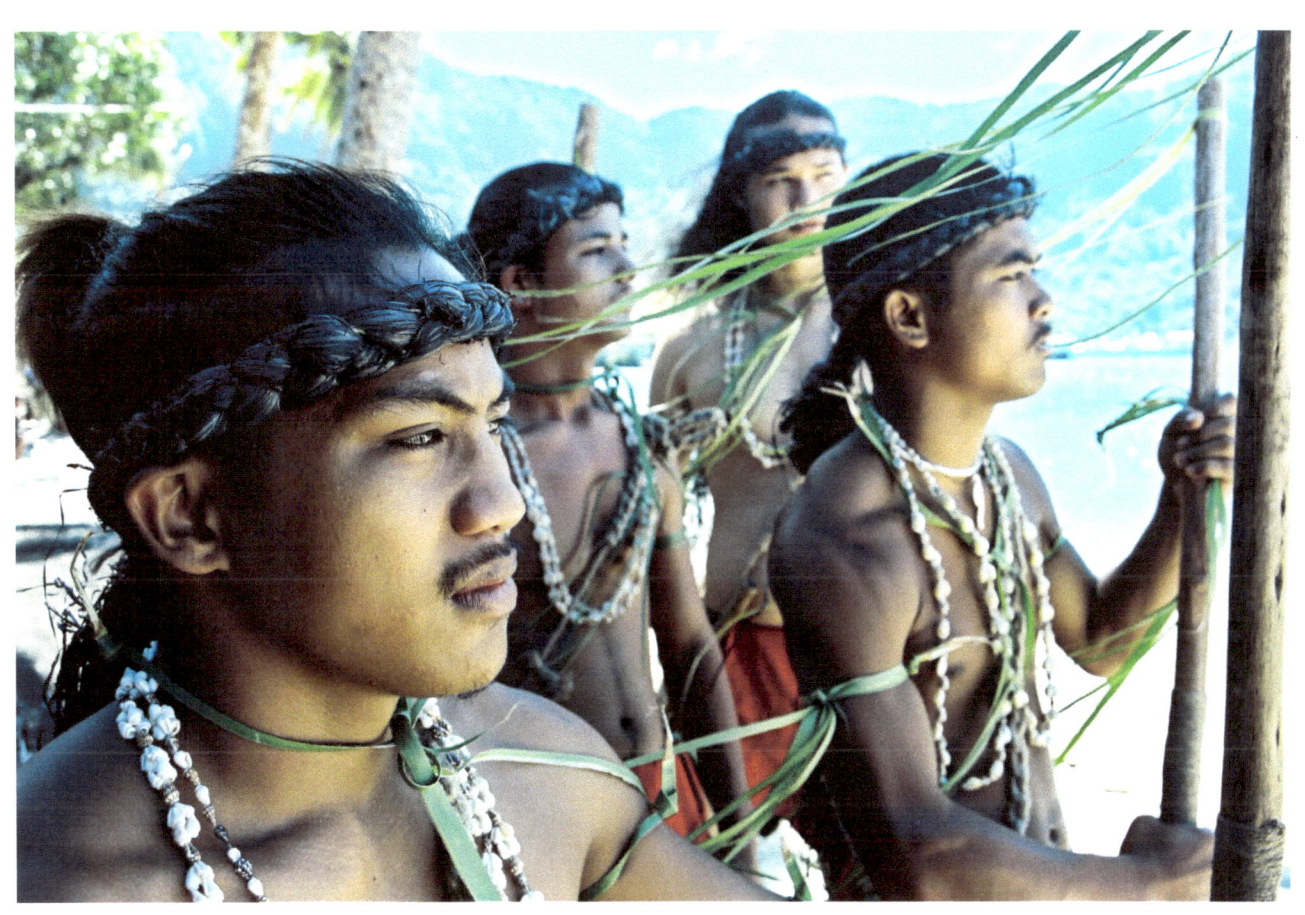

Members of the Guam delegation hold an informal concert.

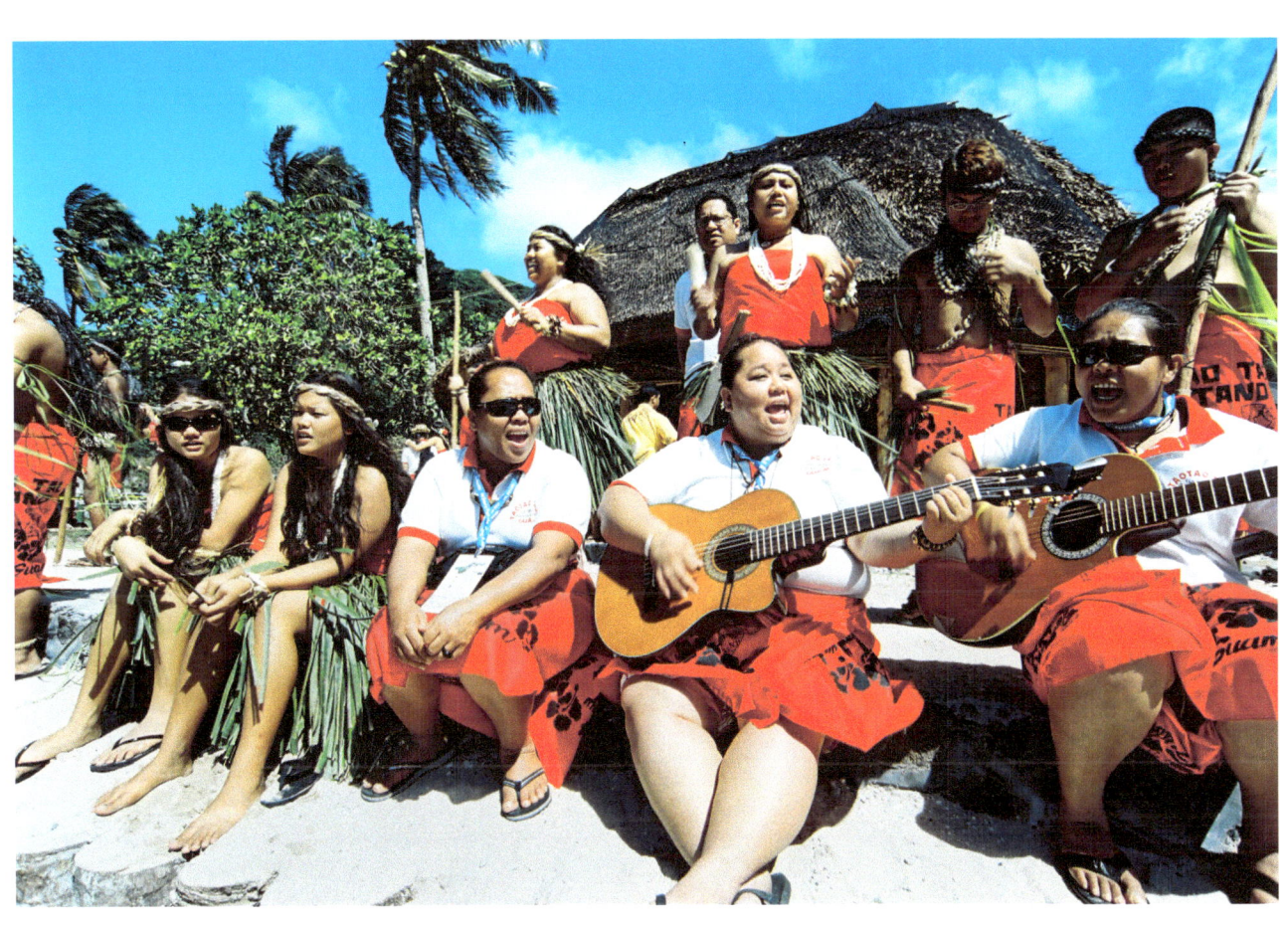

A performer from Guam.

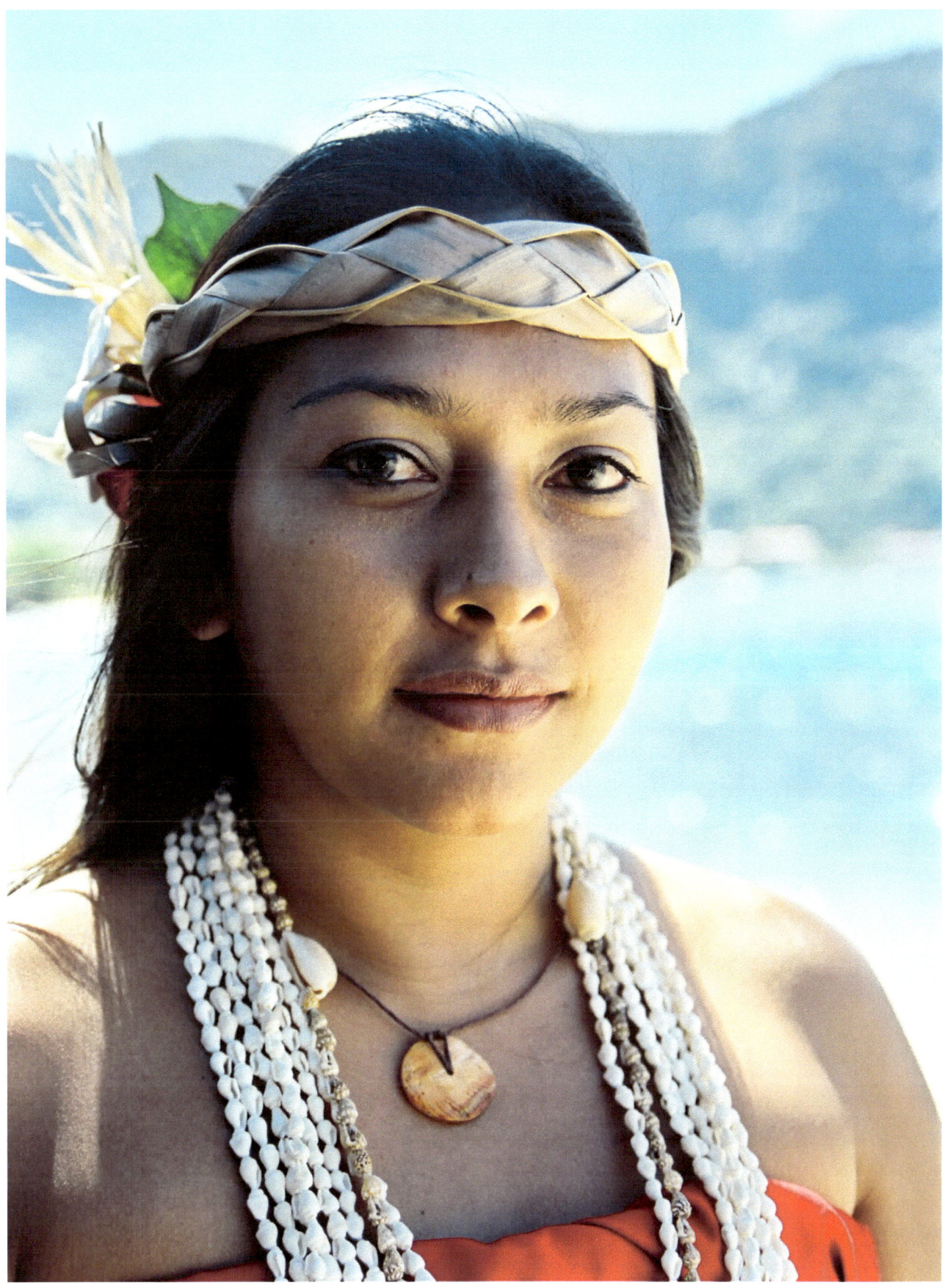

Dancers from Guam.

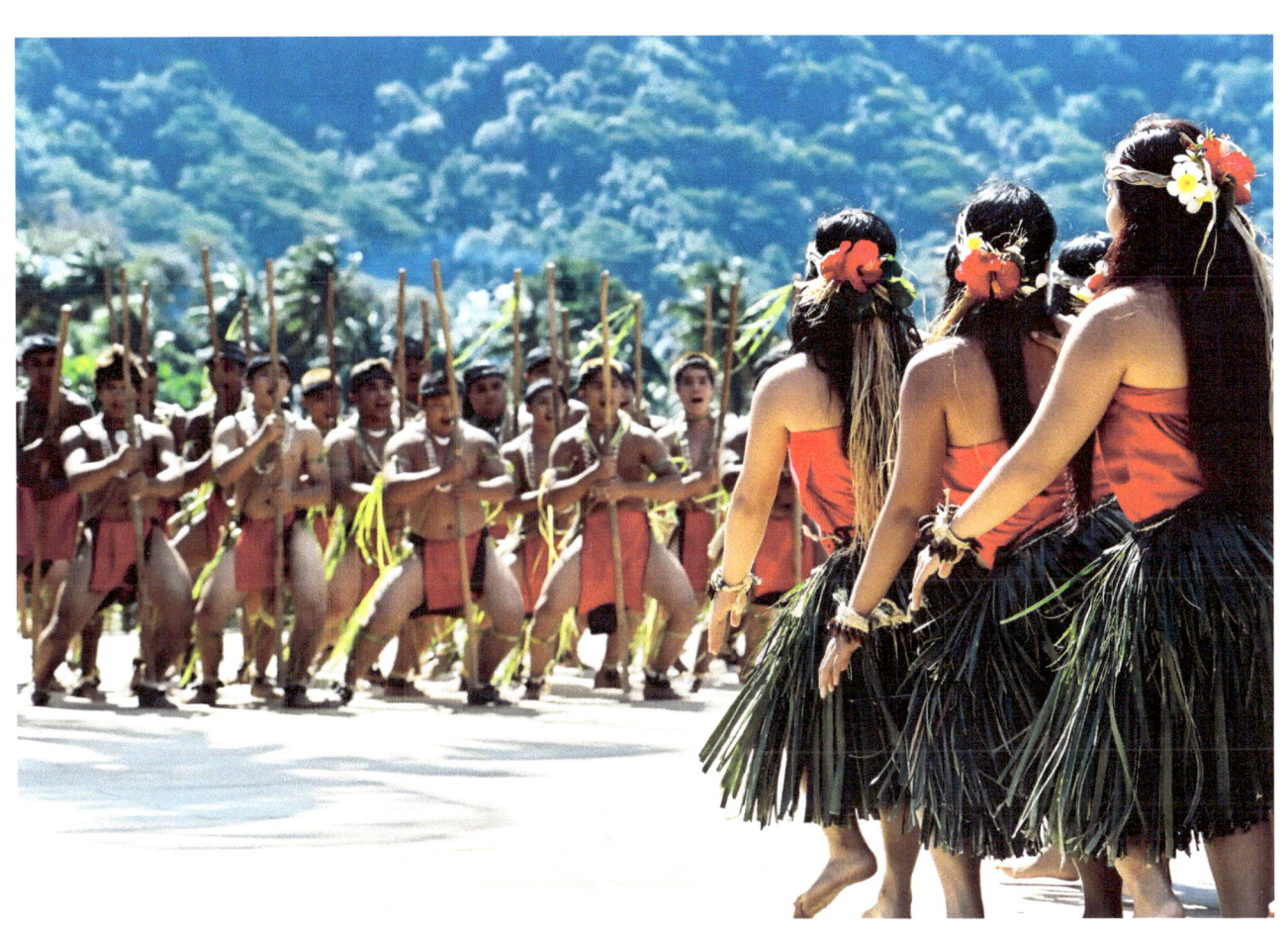

The village of Aua, on Tutuila, hosted the Guam delegation. The program introduced the Guam group to rowing the famous Samoan fautasi racing boats.

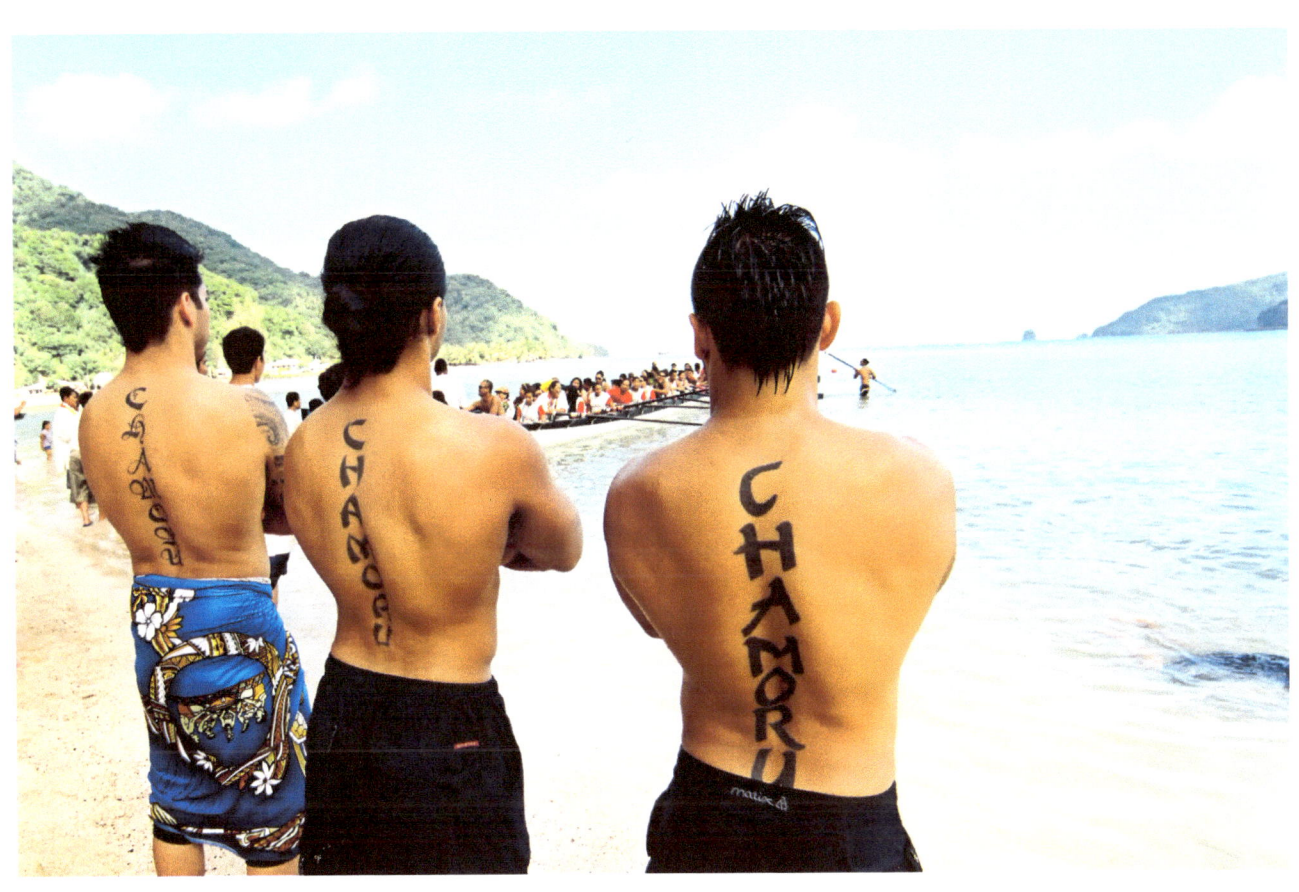

A Guam dancer aboard one of Aua Village's fautasi boats.

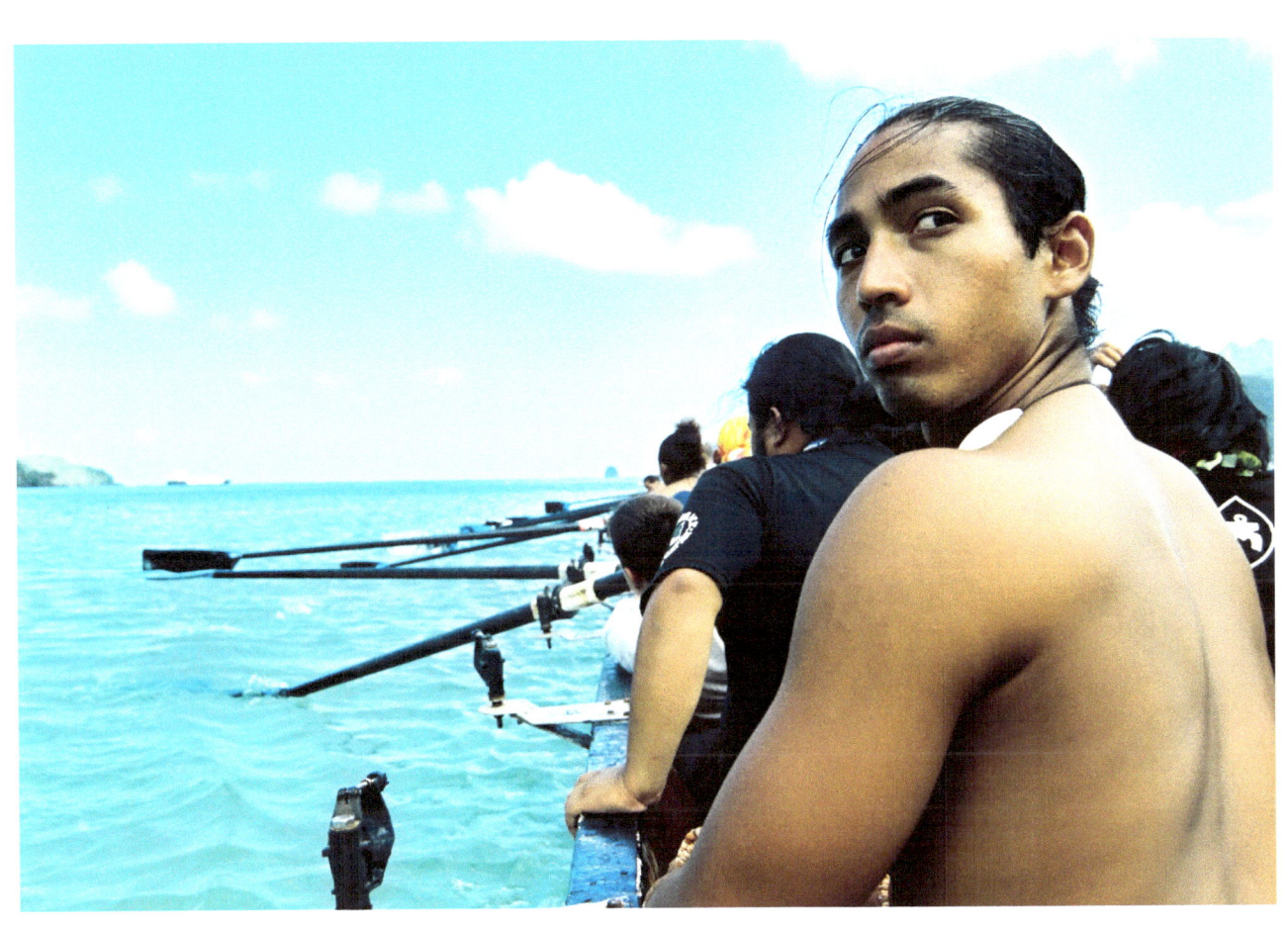

Guam dancers performed for their Samoan hosts at a welcome party in Aua Village.

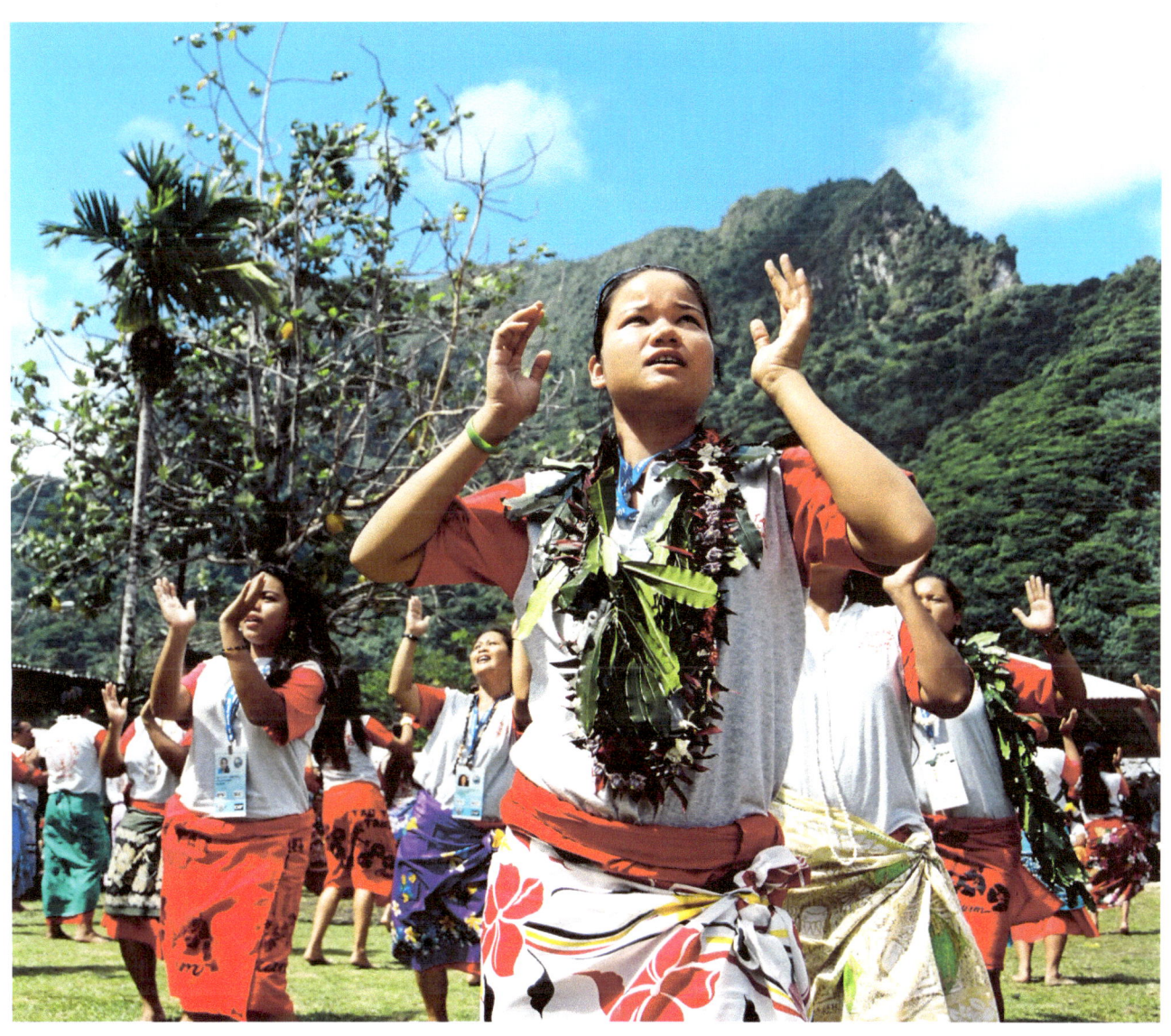

Dancers from Hawaii.

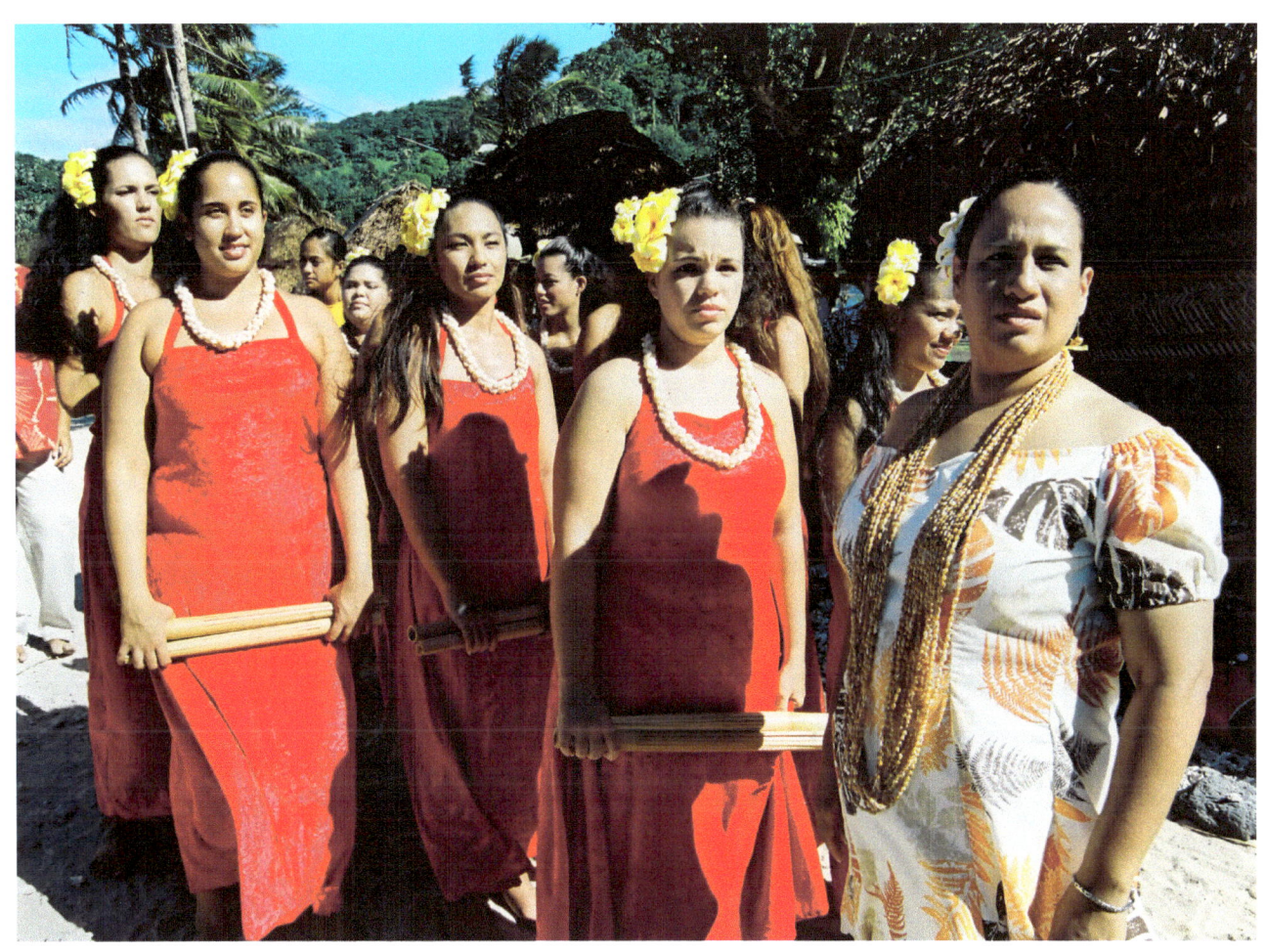

Dancers from Hawaii were members of the hula group Halau Mohala ʻIlima,
which has performed at previous Festivals.

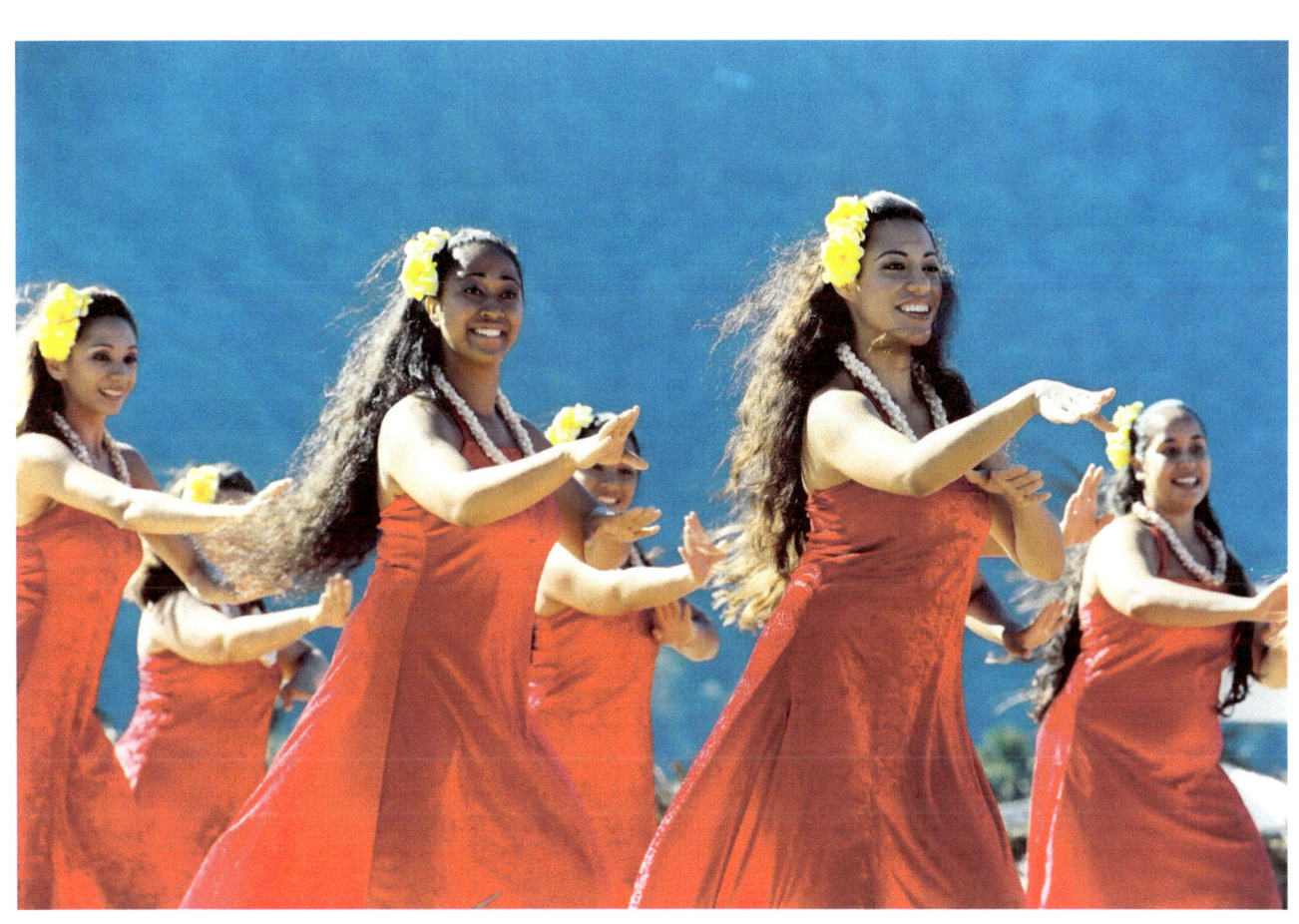

The Hawaii group showed Festival-goers how to make kapa, the Hawaiian version of tapa, a fabric made from plant materials.

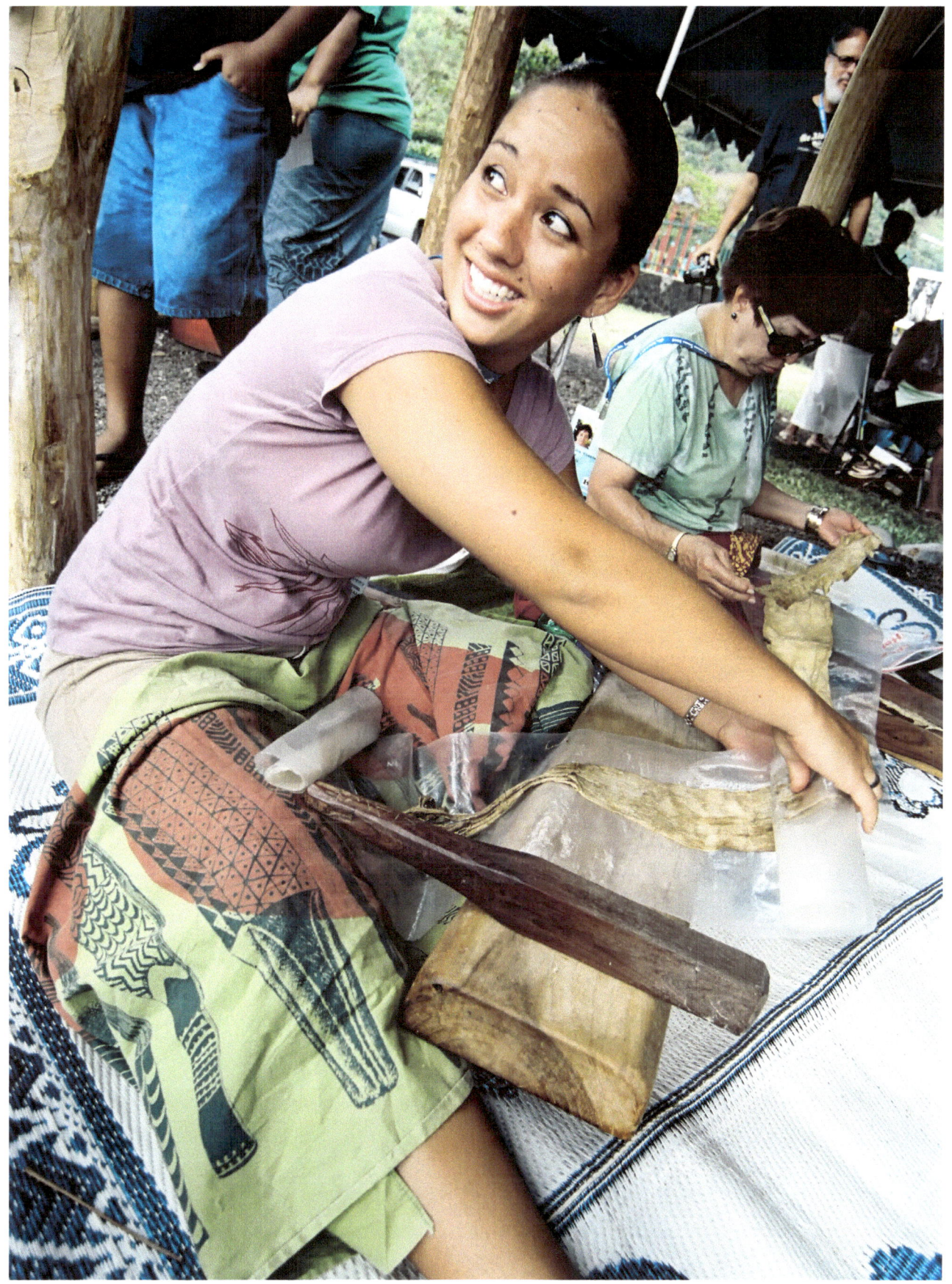

Dancers from Hawaii's Halau Mohala 'Ilima wait to go on stage.

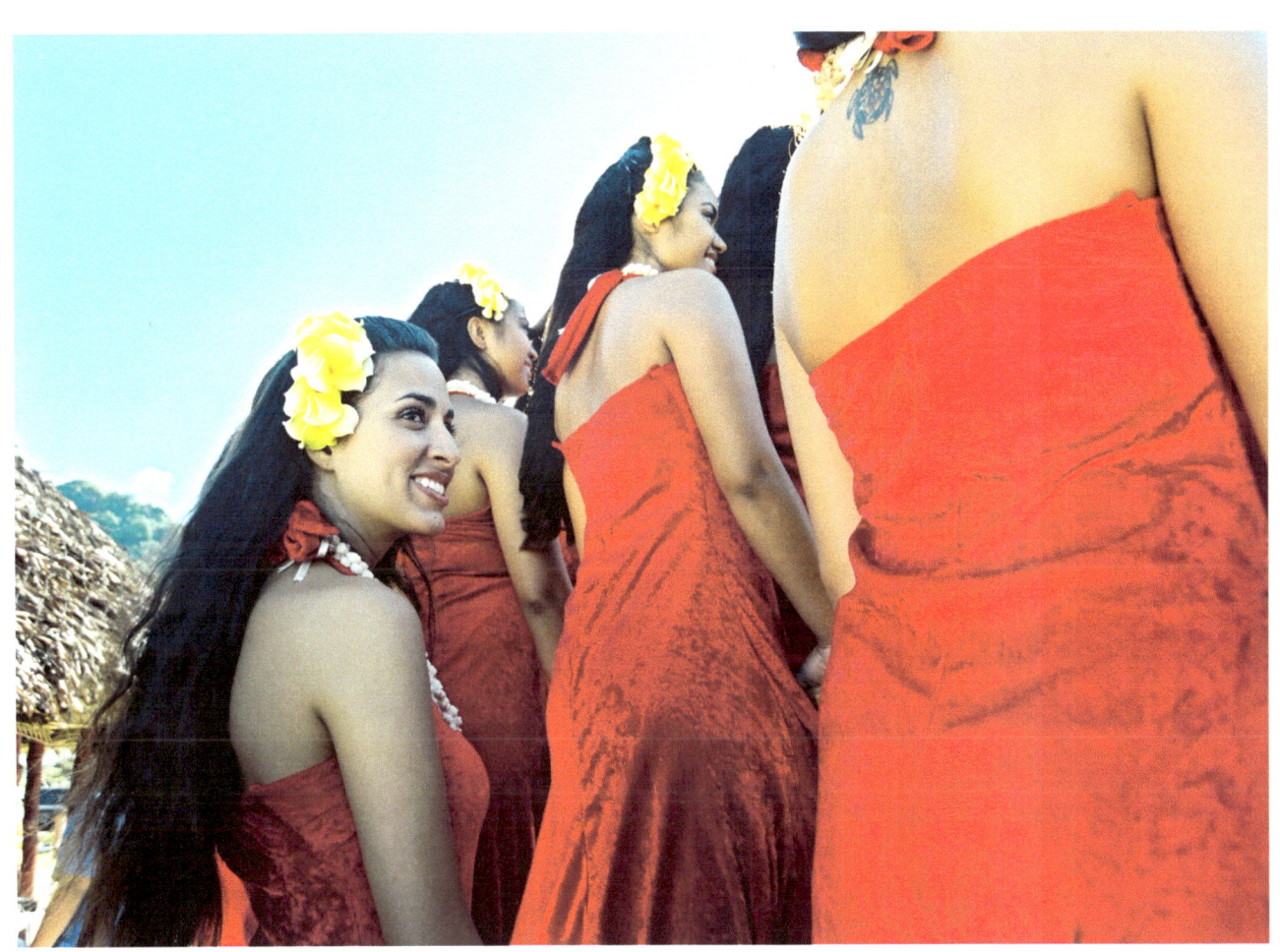

Dancers from Kiribati.

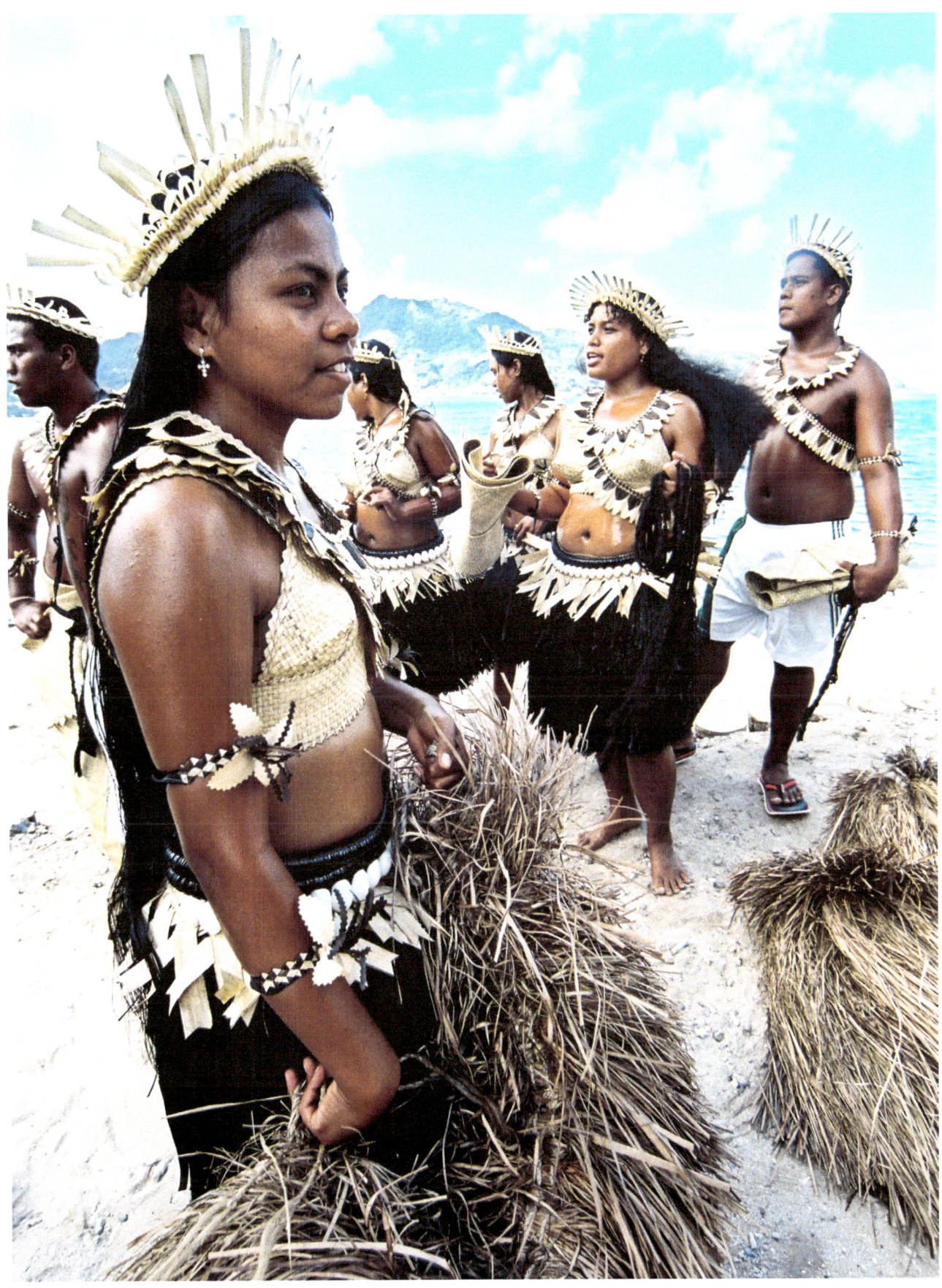

Performers get used to waiting at the Festival, as this young man from Kiribati learns.

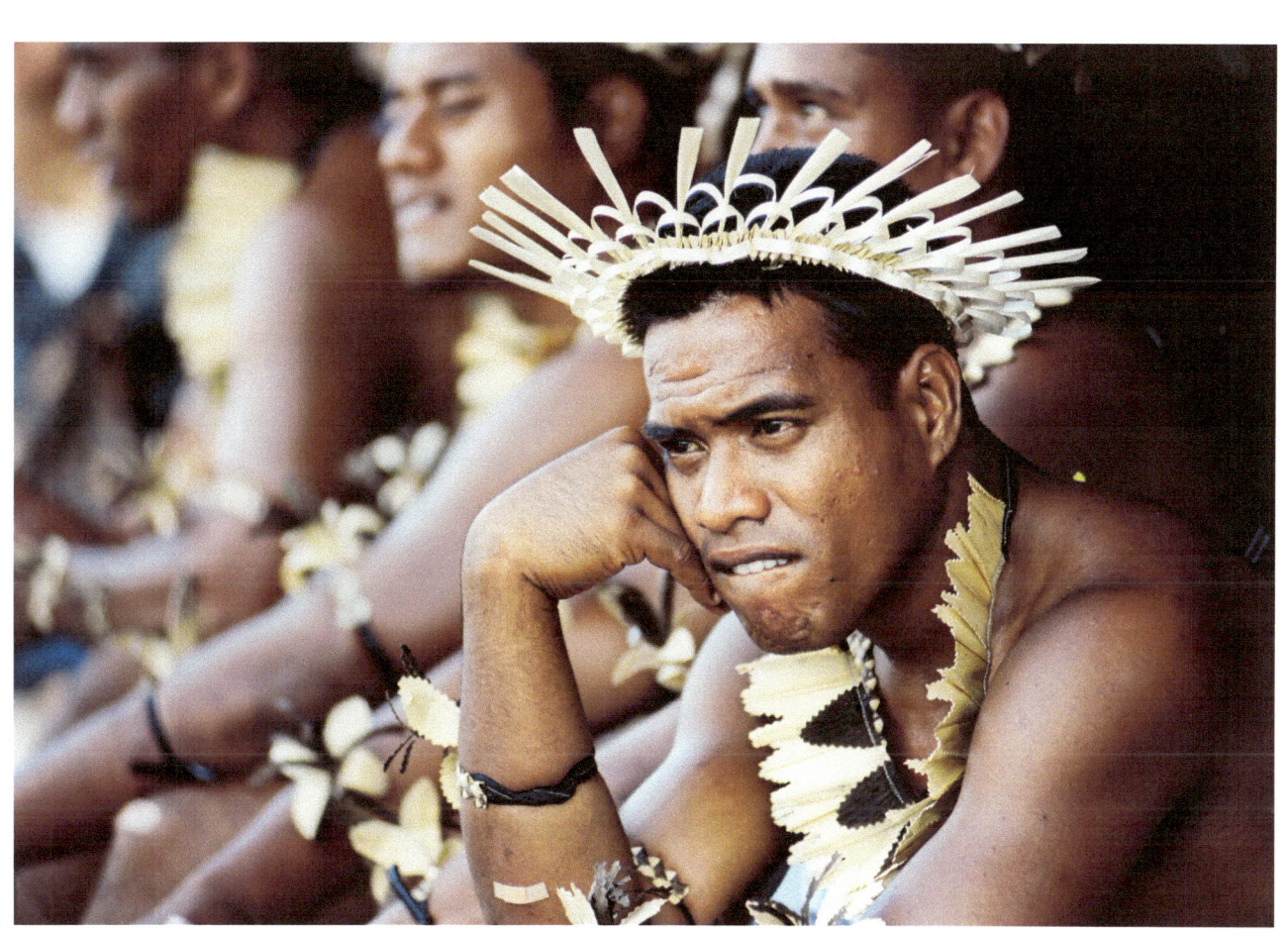

A dancer from Kiribati.

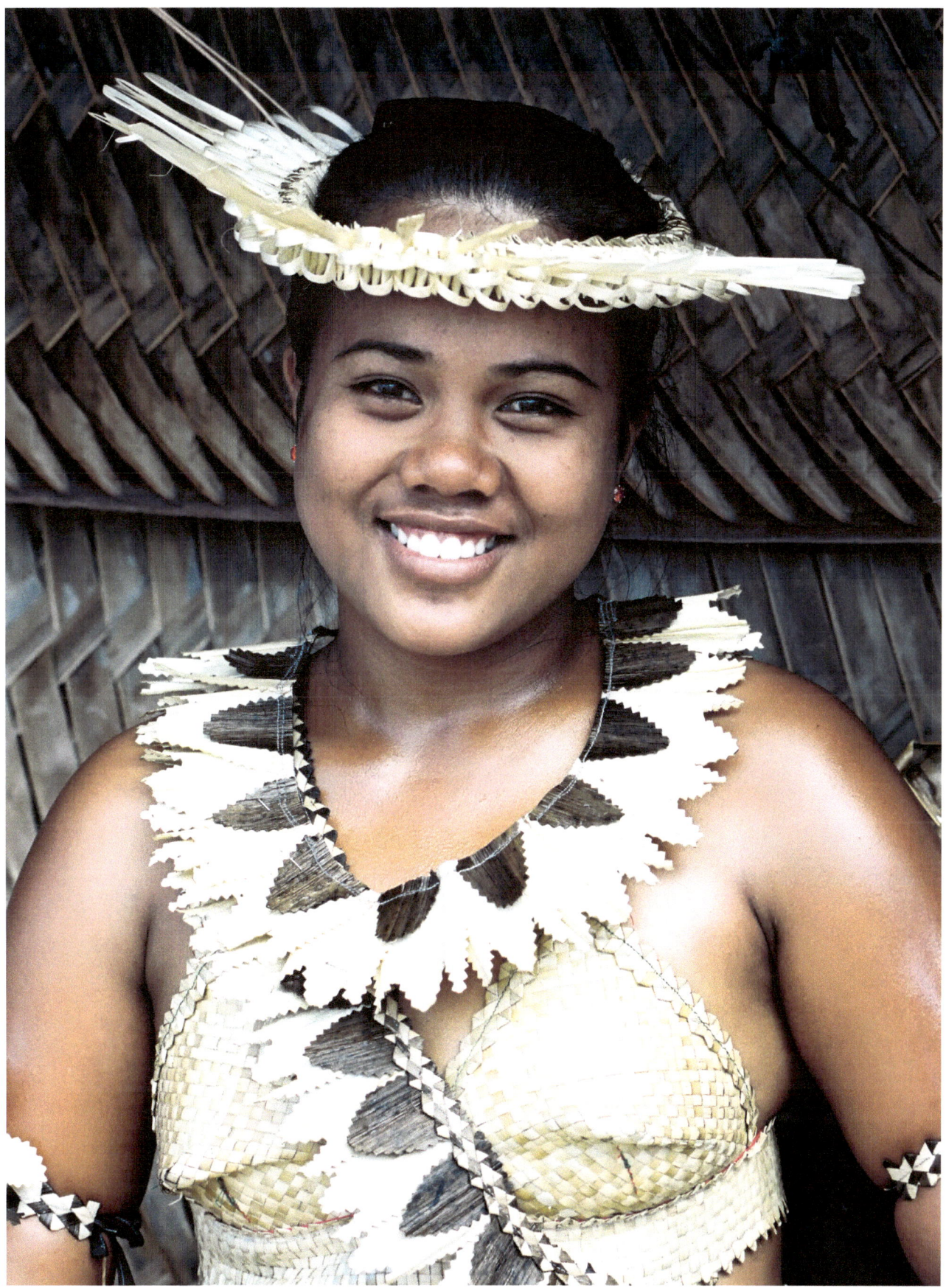

An American Samoan assigned to the Kiribati group helps by applying coconut oil to a dancer.

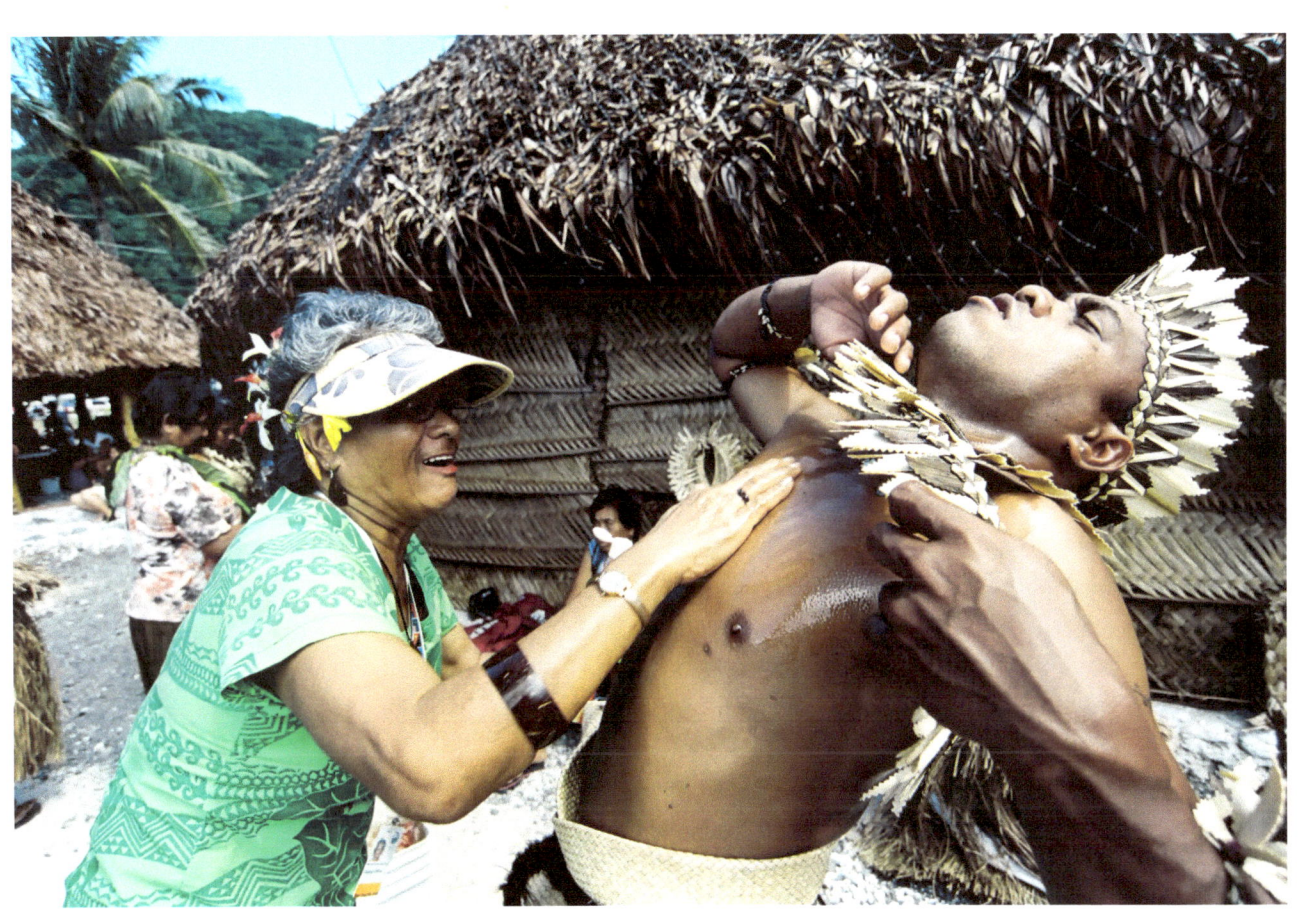

The Kiribati troupe on stage at the Festival.

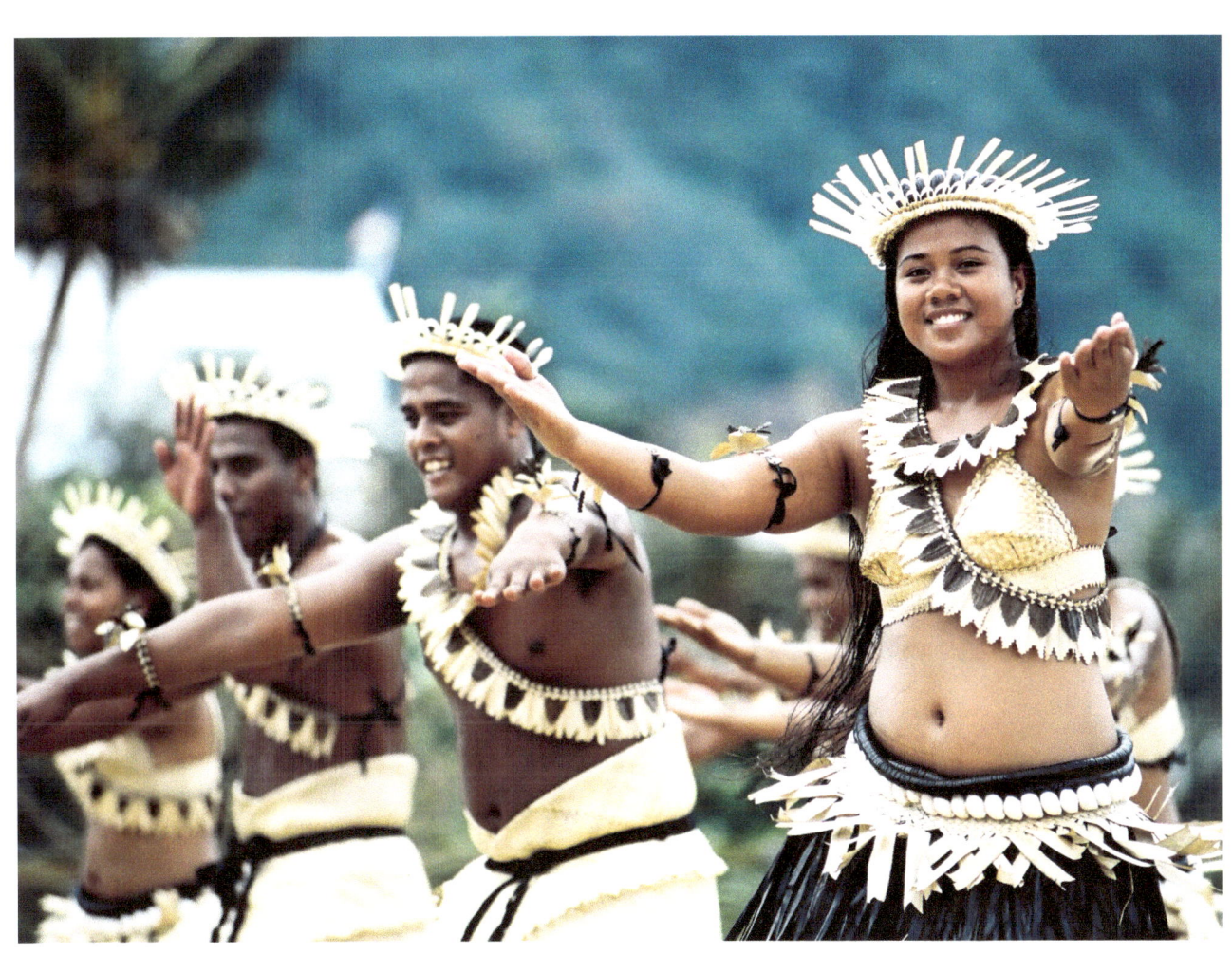

Dancers from New Caledonia.

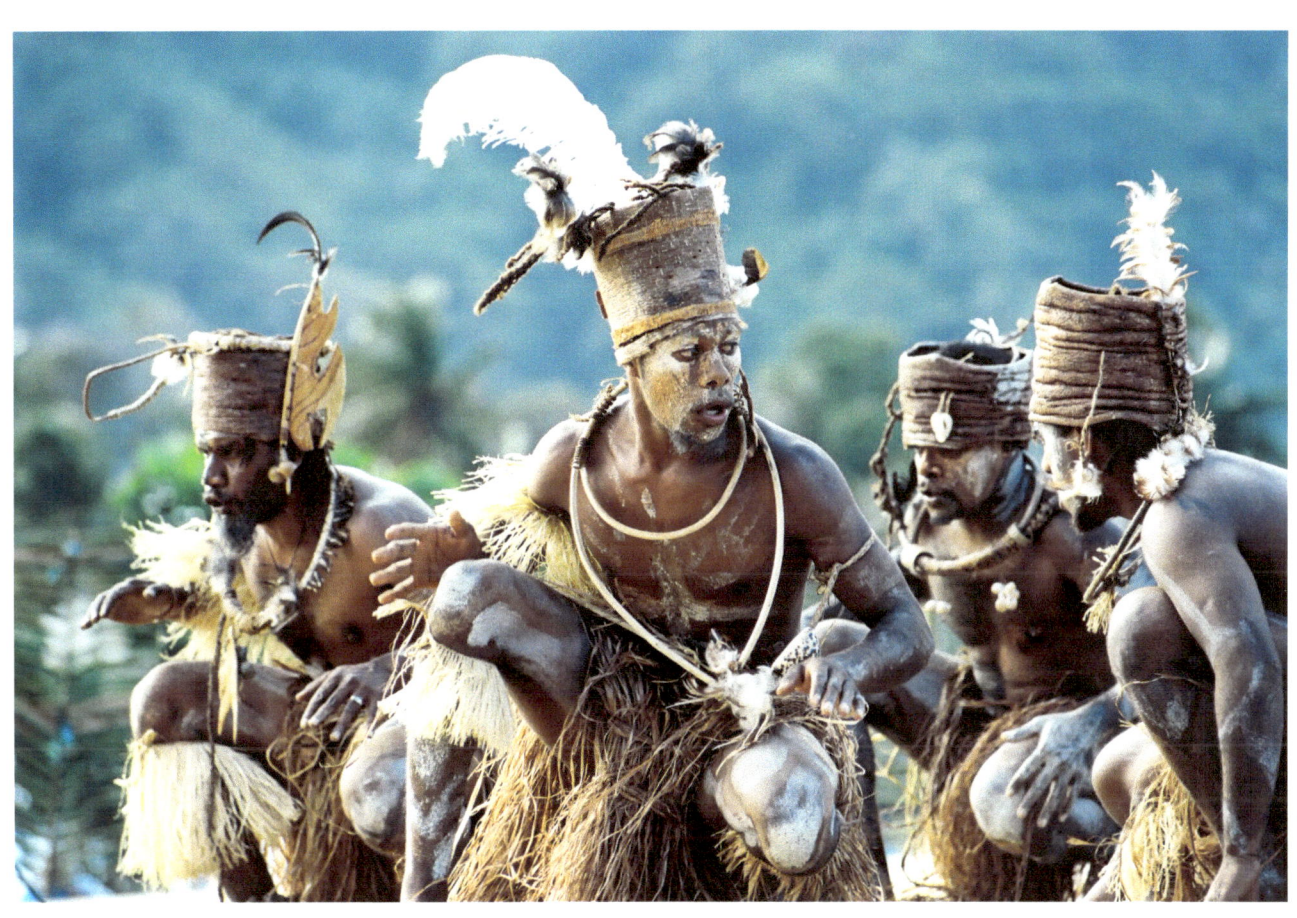

A dancer from New Caledonia waits on stage to begin a performance.

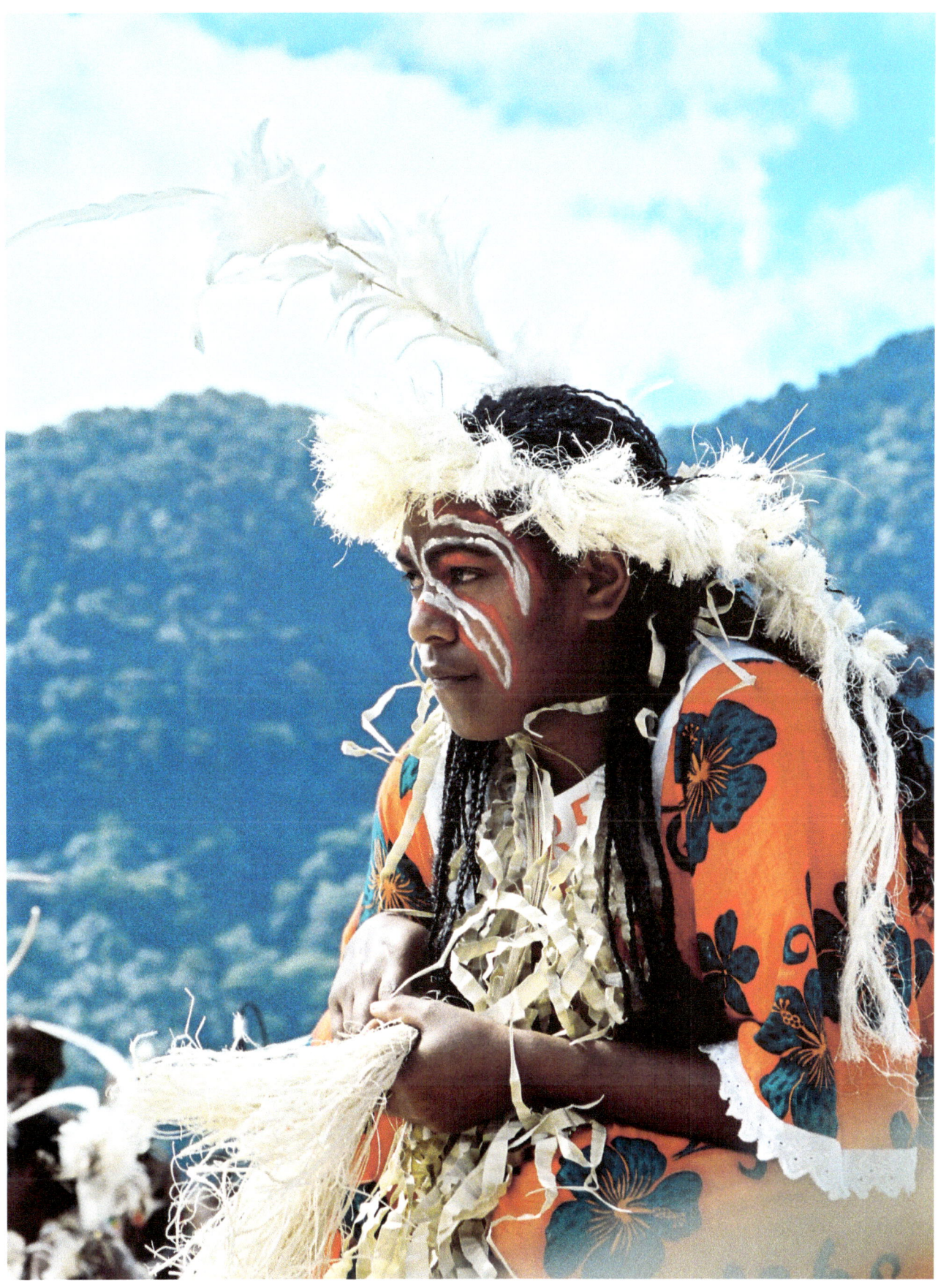

A New Caledonian dancer in traditional attire.

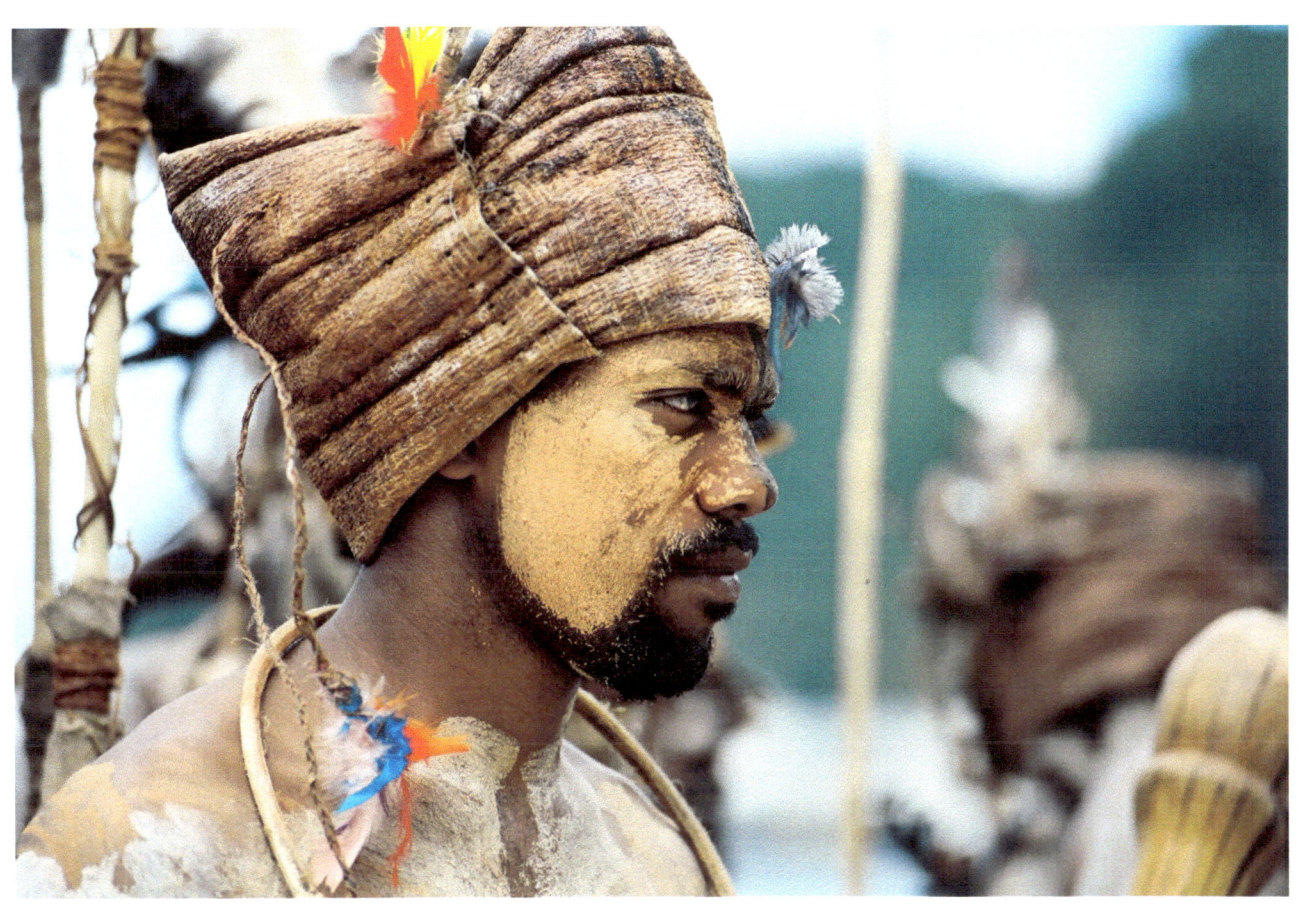

The popular New Zealand (Aotearoa) group performs at the Utulei Beach venue.

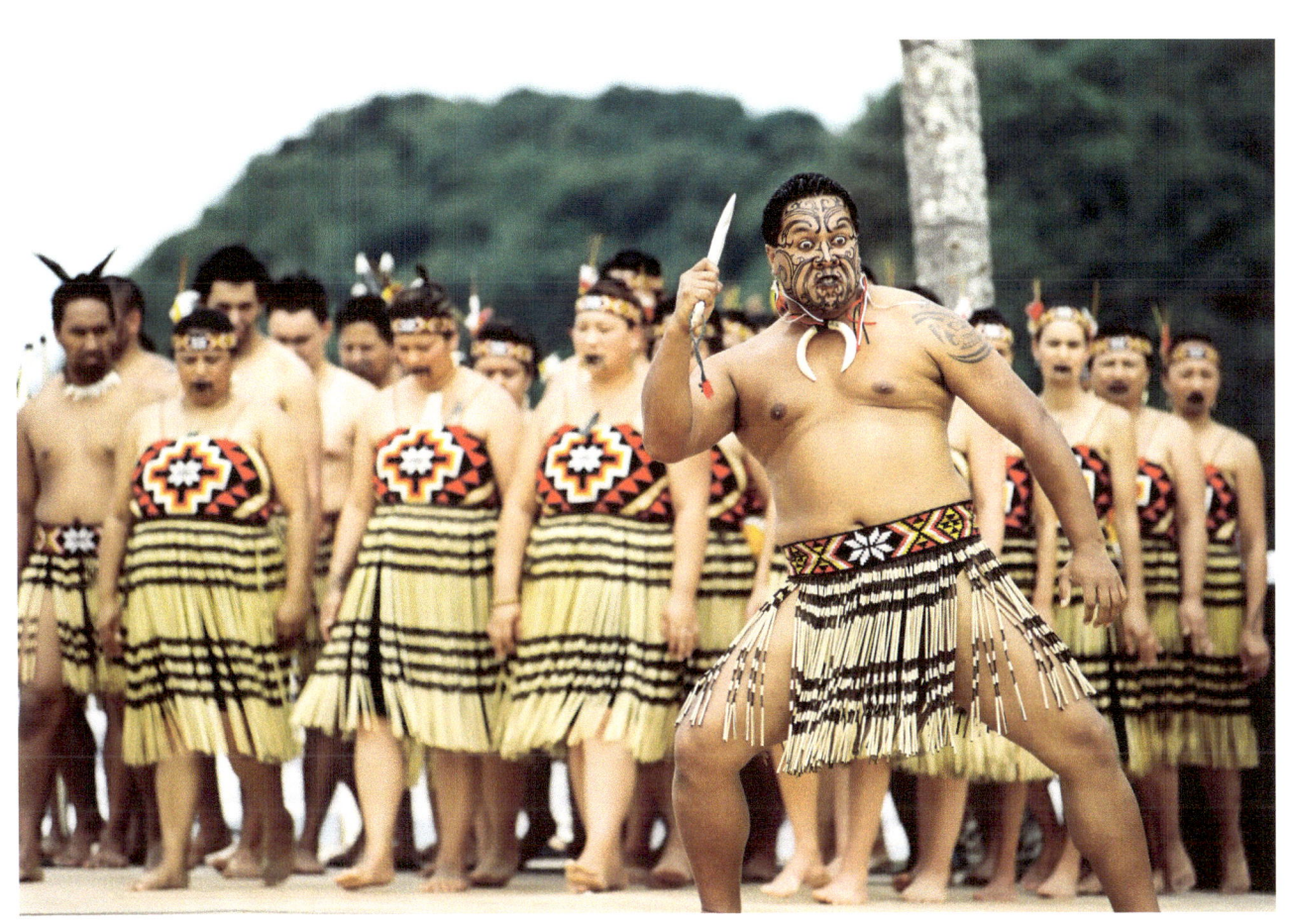

Three members of the New Zealand (Aotearoa) troupe relax in the shade of a fale.

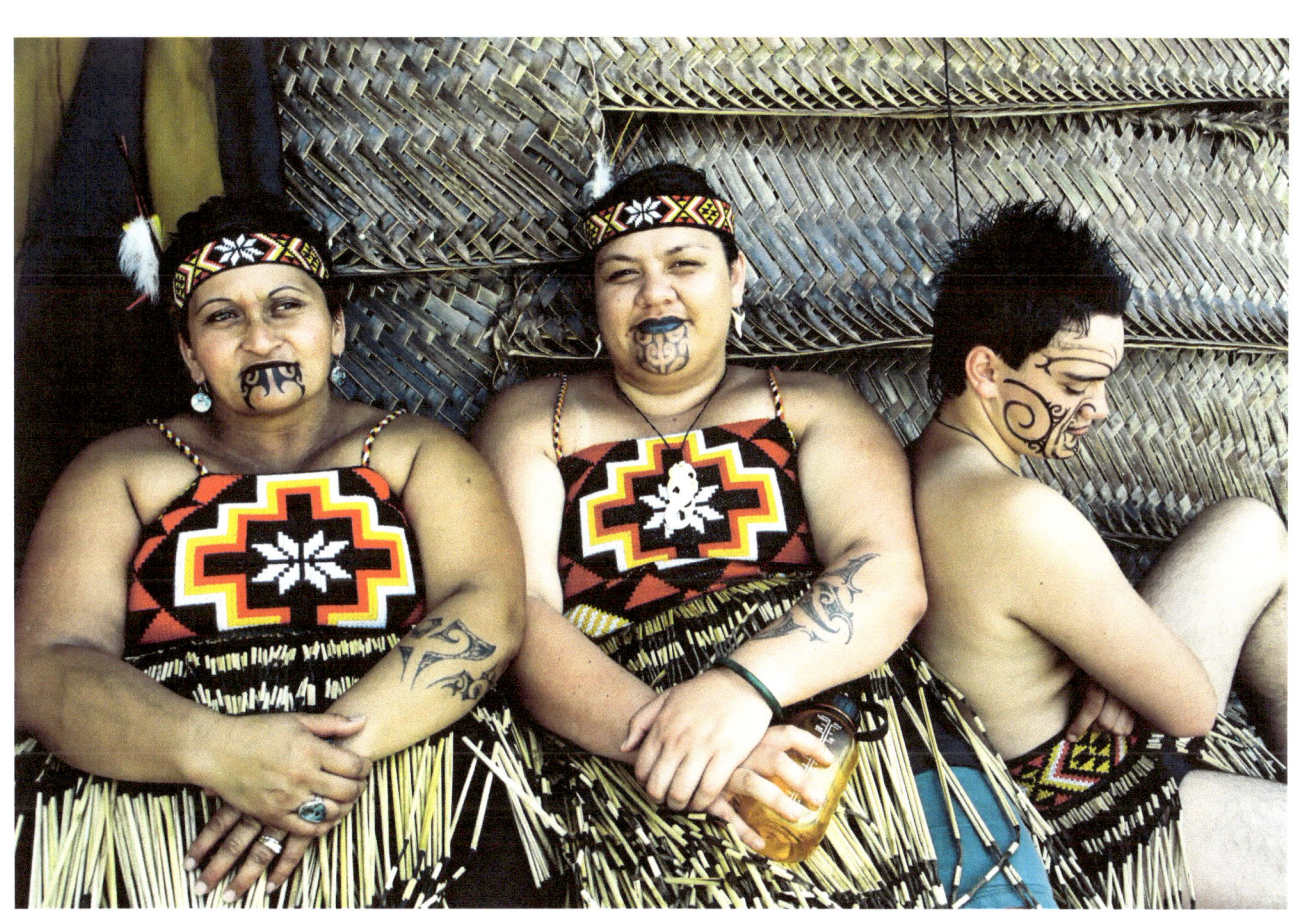

A dancer from Niue wears the bright yellow shell lei that are popular on her island.

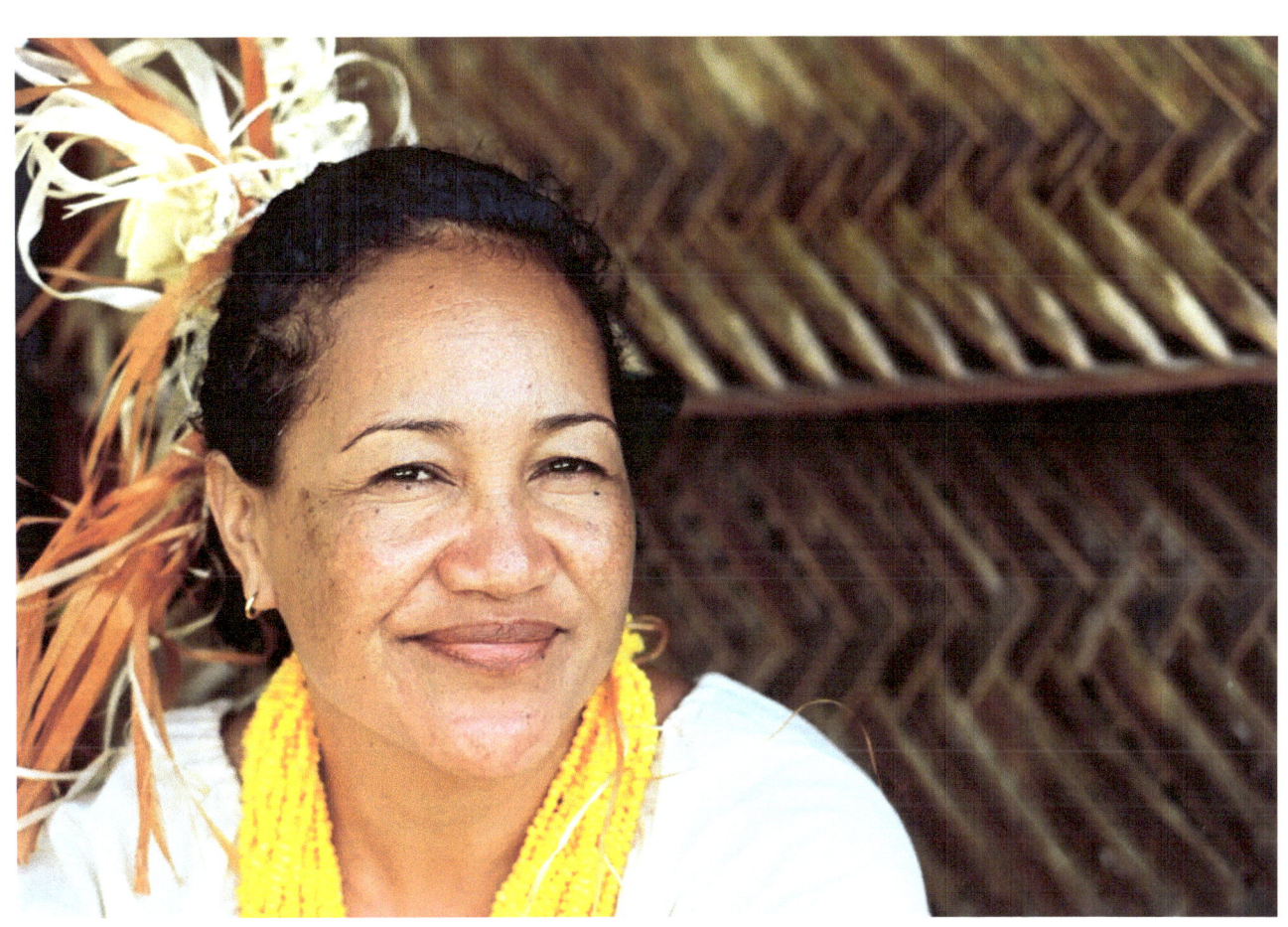

Dancers from Niue, a small island state affiliated with New Zealand.

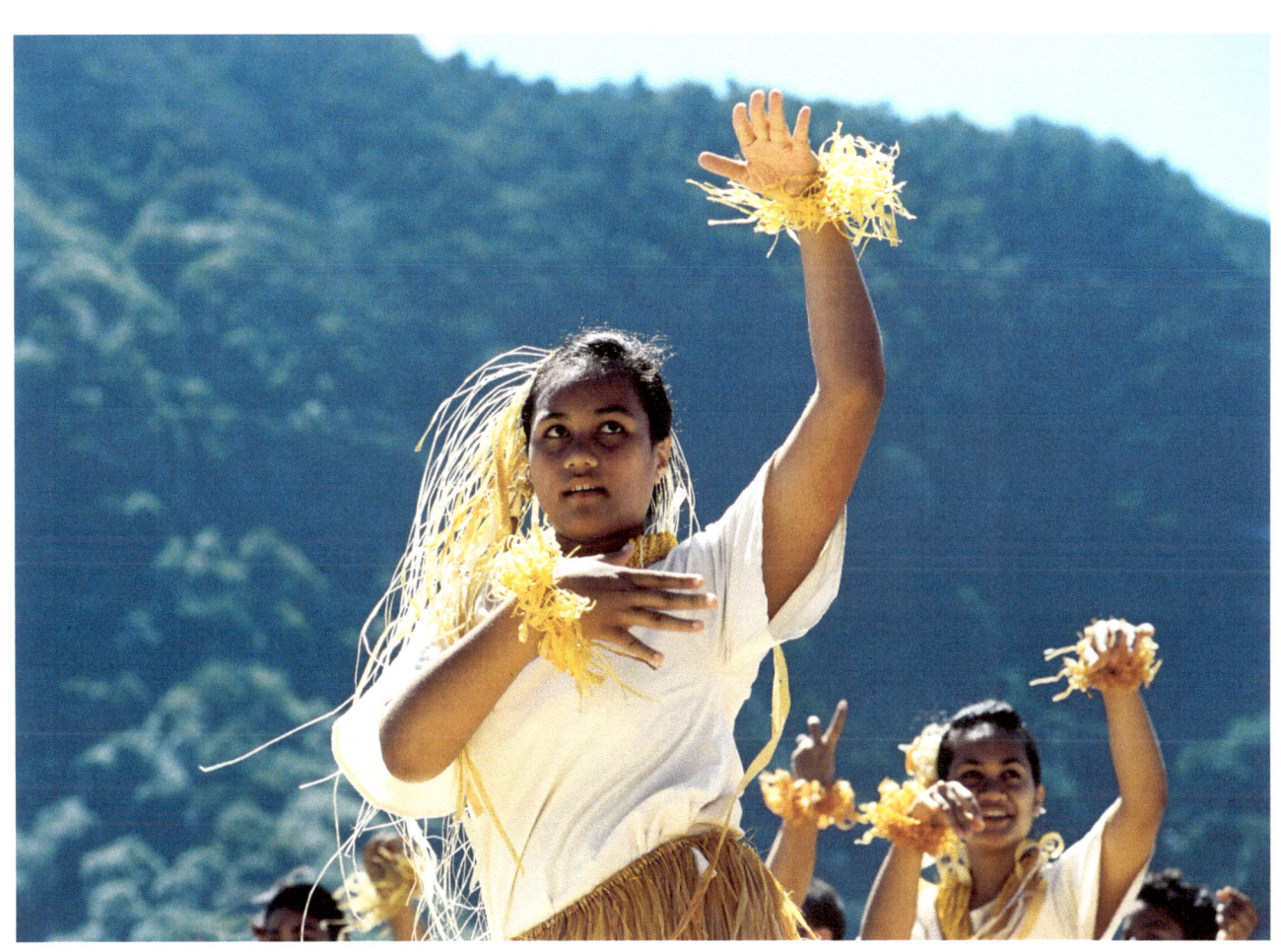

Dancers from Niue.

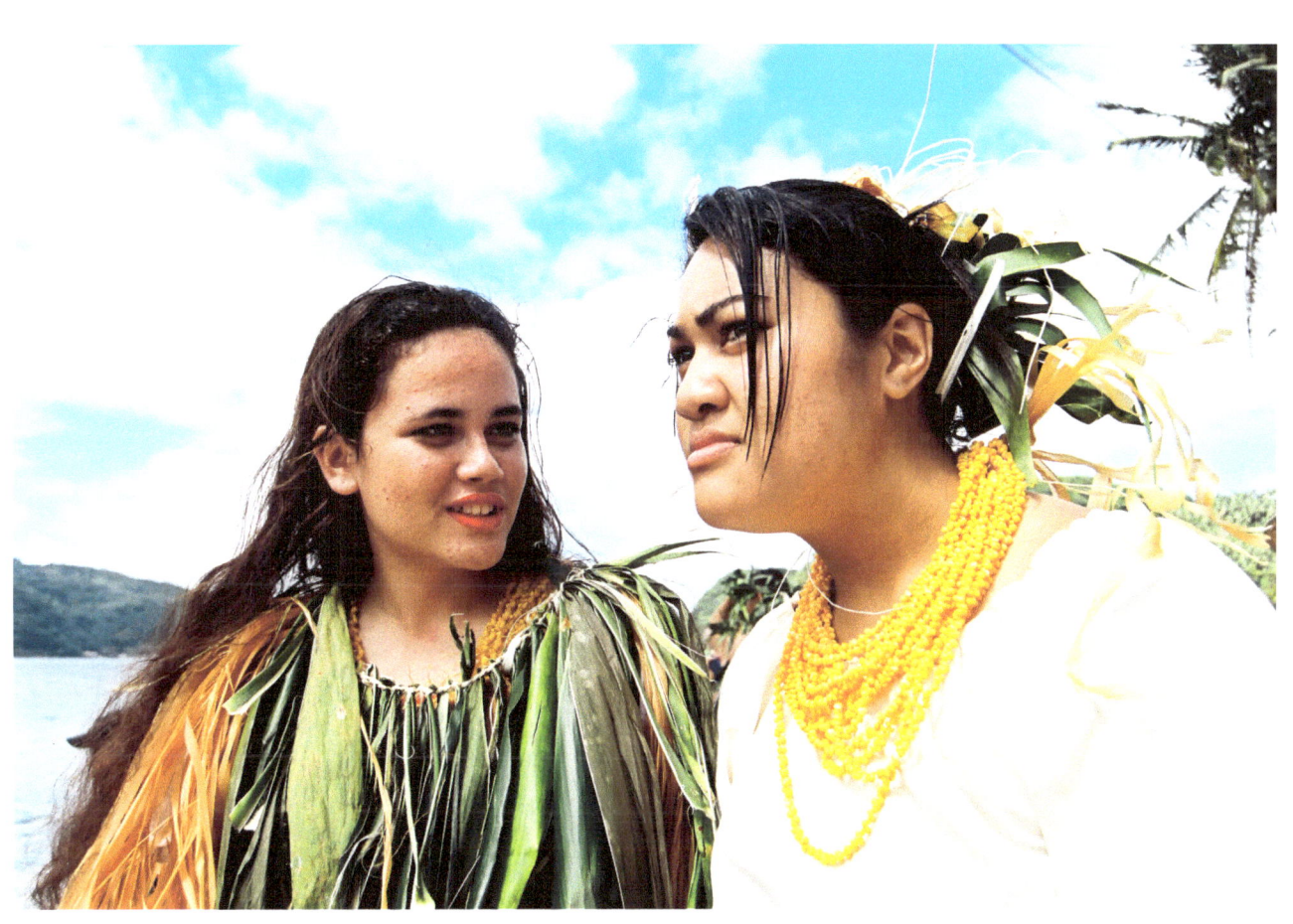

Niuean performers keep out of the intense tropical sun.

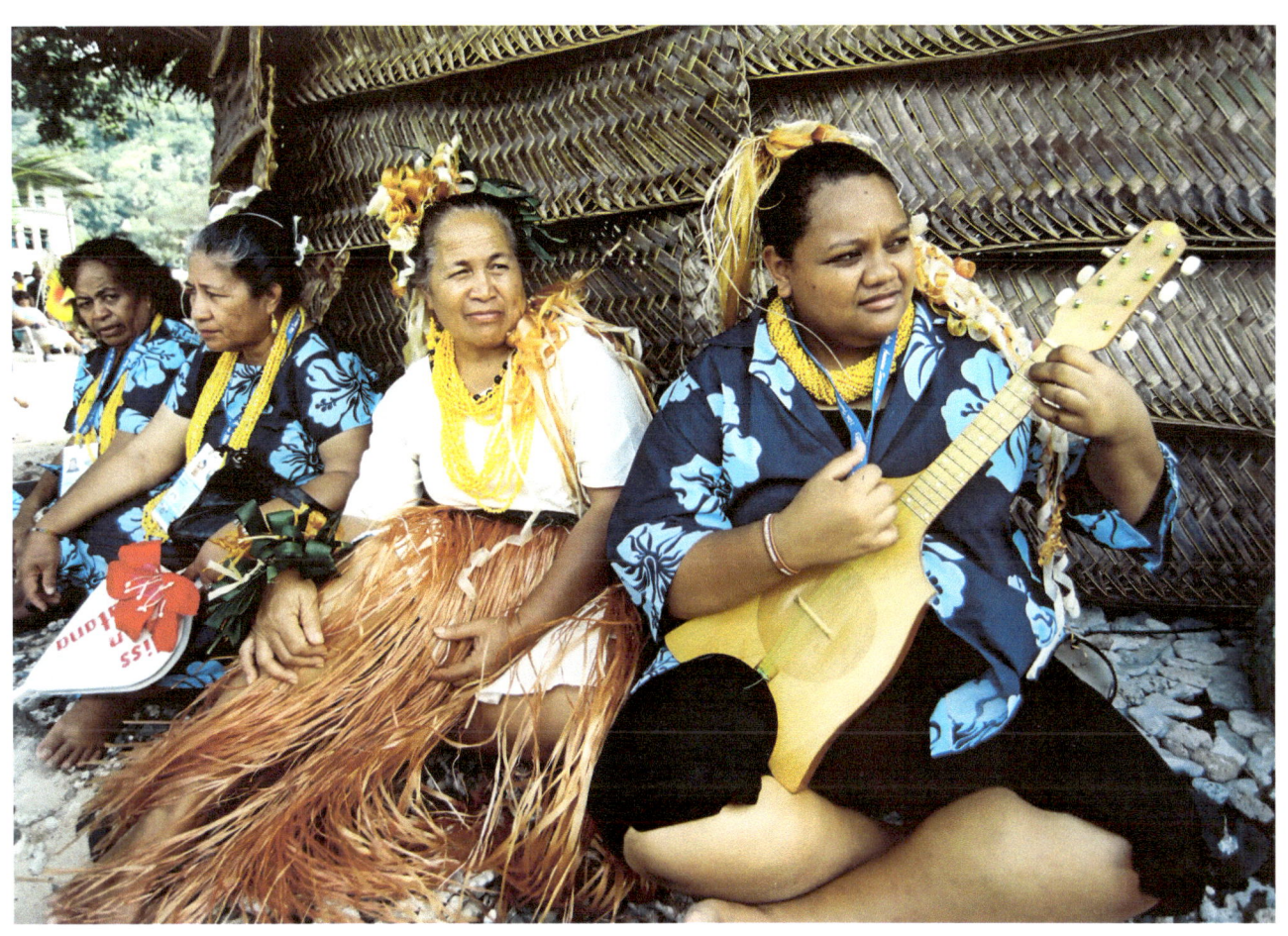

This is the only dancer from Norfolk Island, which is part of Australia. Many Norfolk residents are descendants of Tahitians and mutineers from the HMS Bounty.

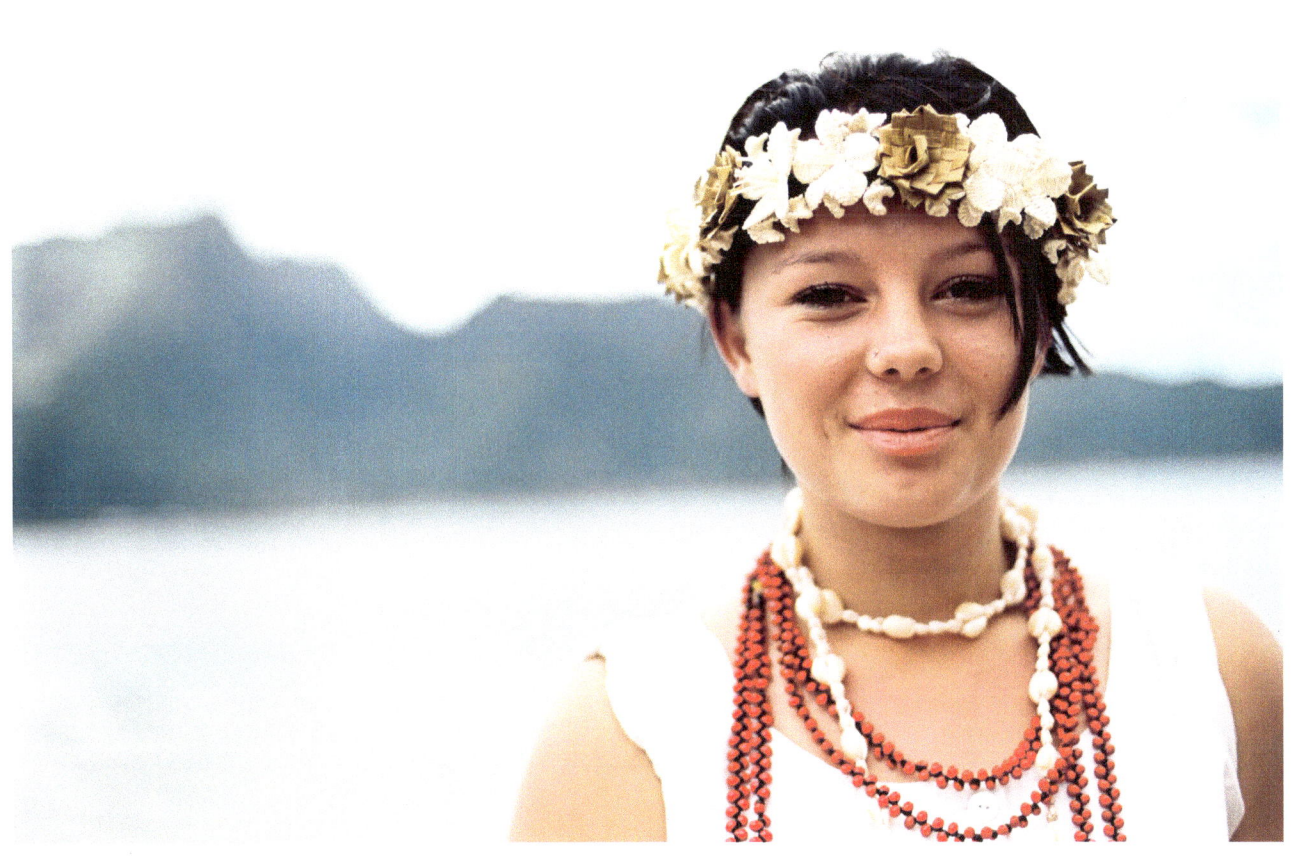

Dancers from Palau.

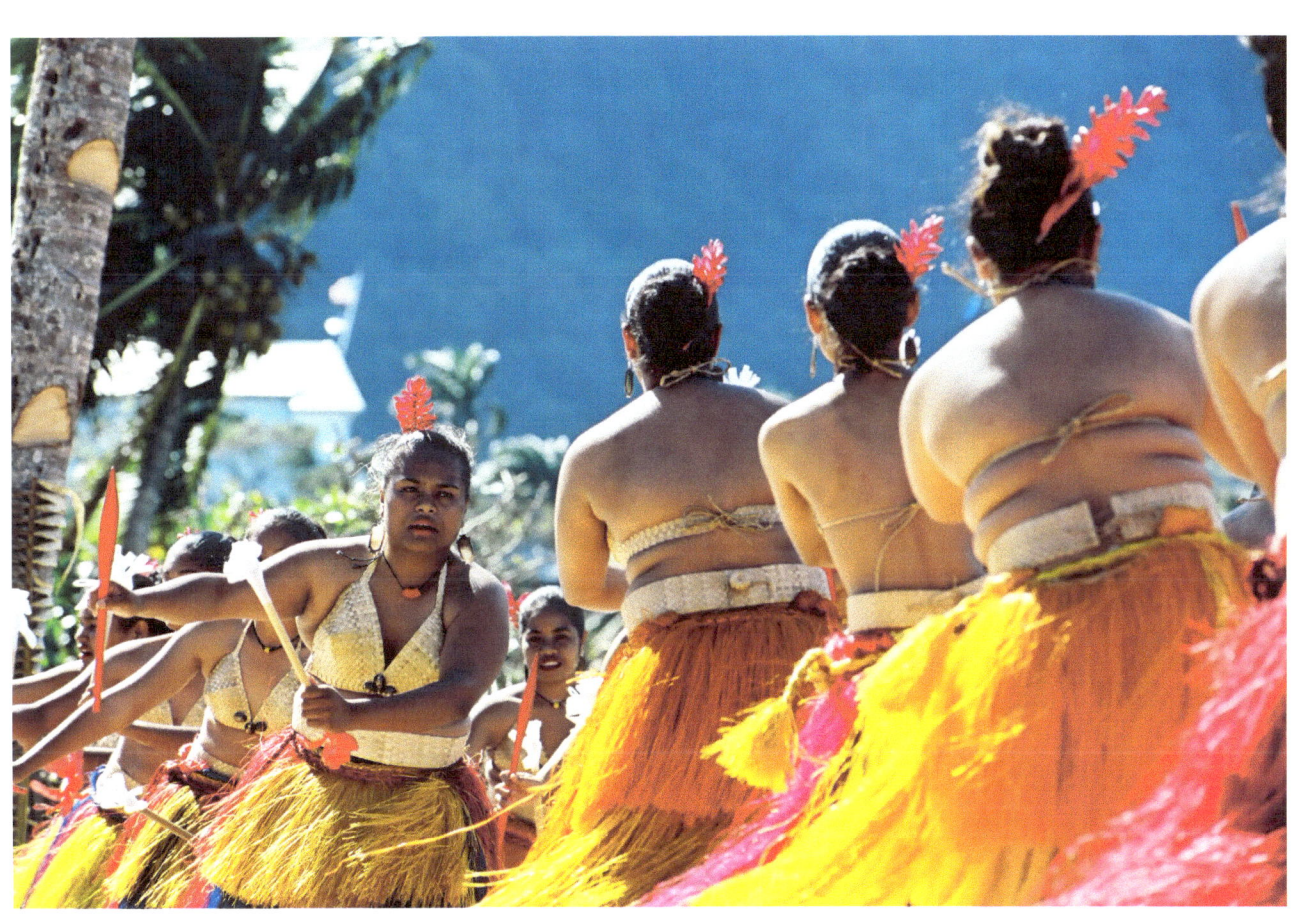

A dancer from Palau wears a traditional women's necklace made from local clay.

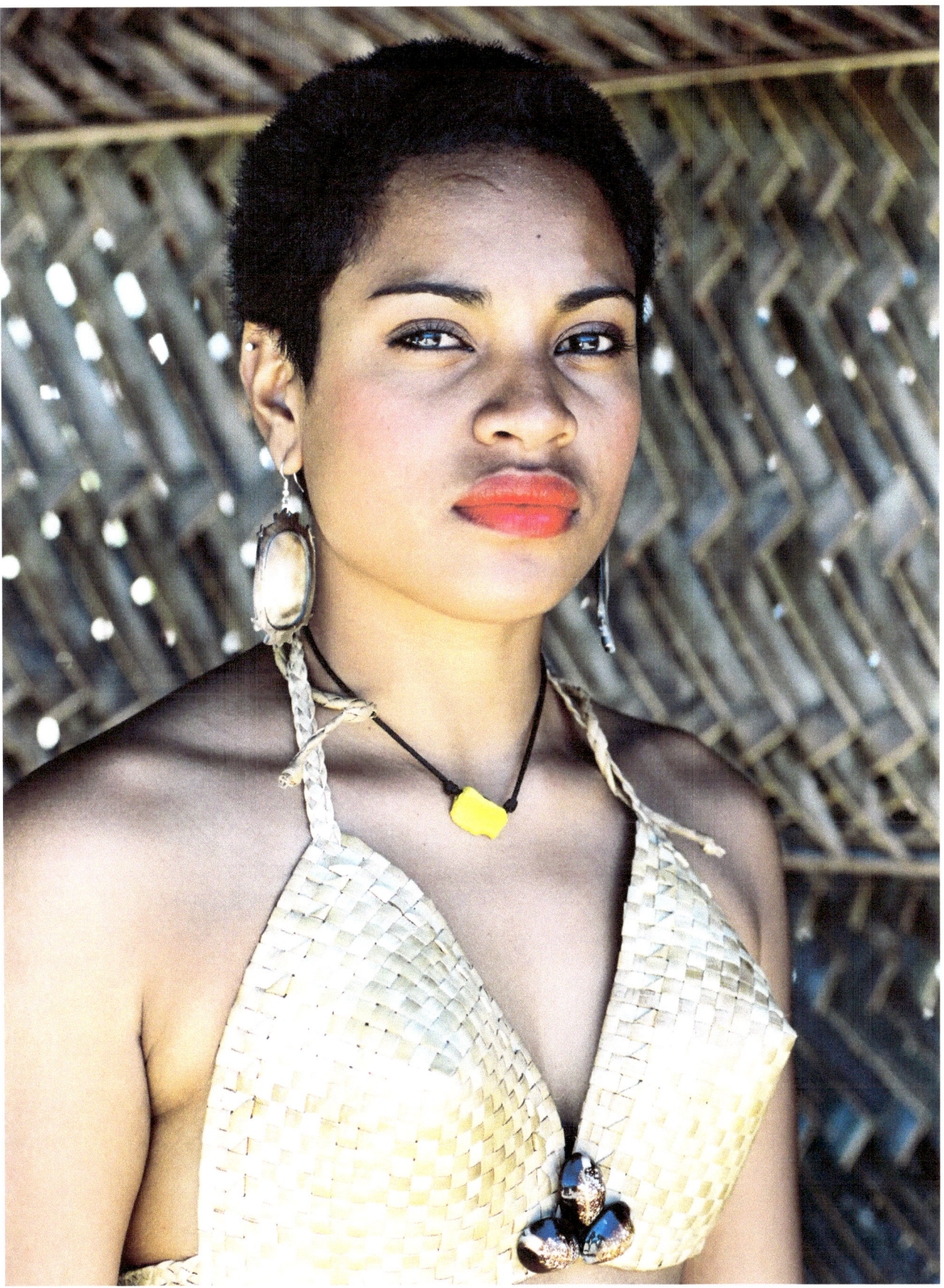

Palauan dancers relax during a break between performances.

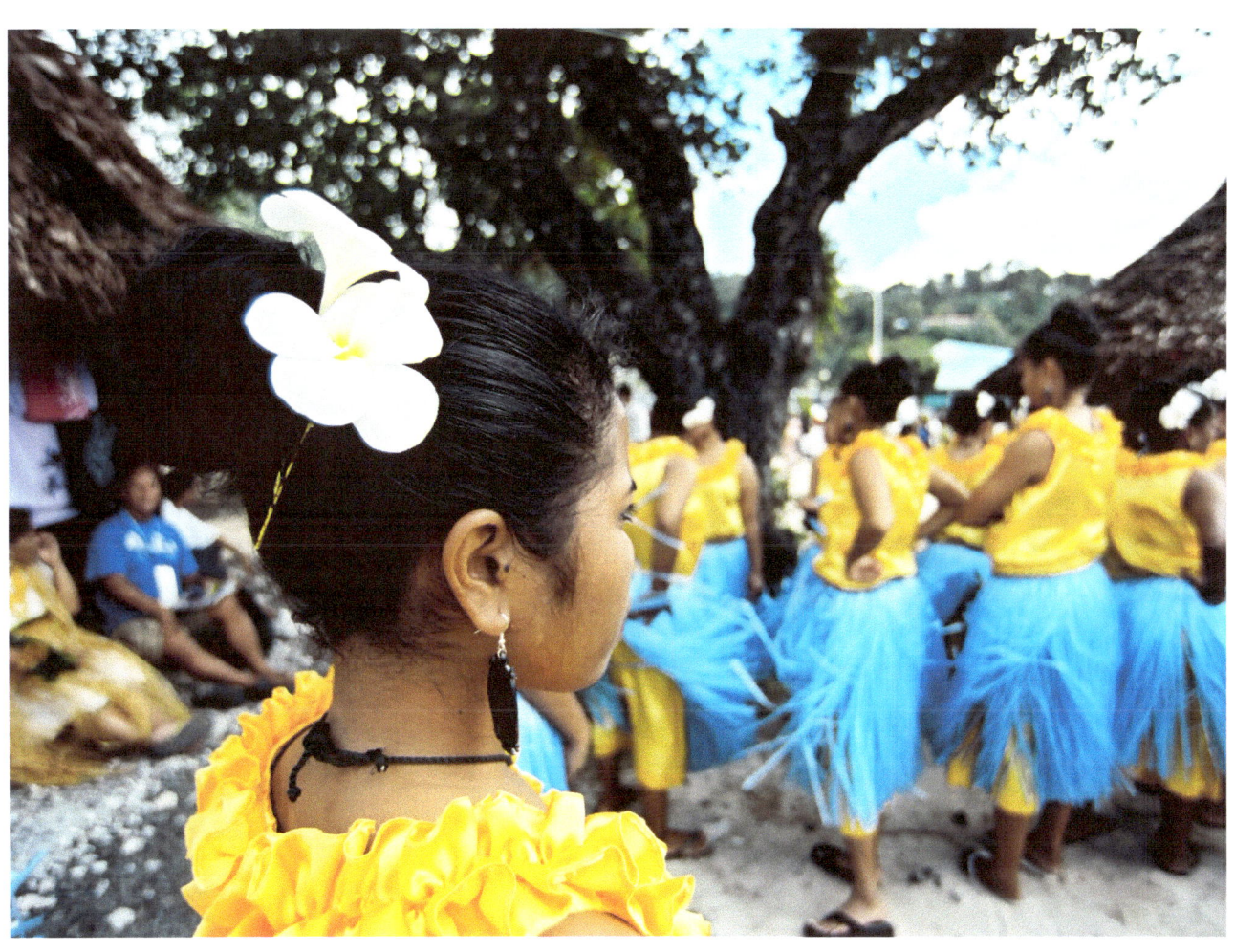

Three performers from Palau wait on the shore of Pago Pago Harbor. The color of their costume is based on the national flag of Palau.

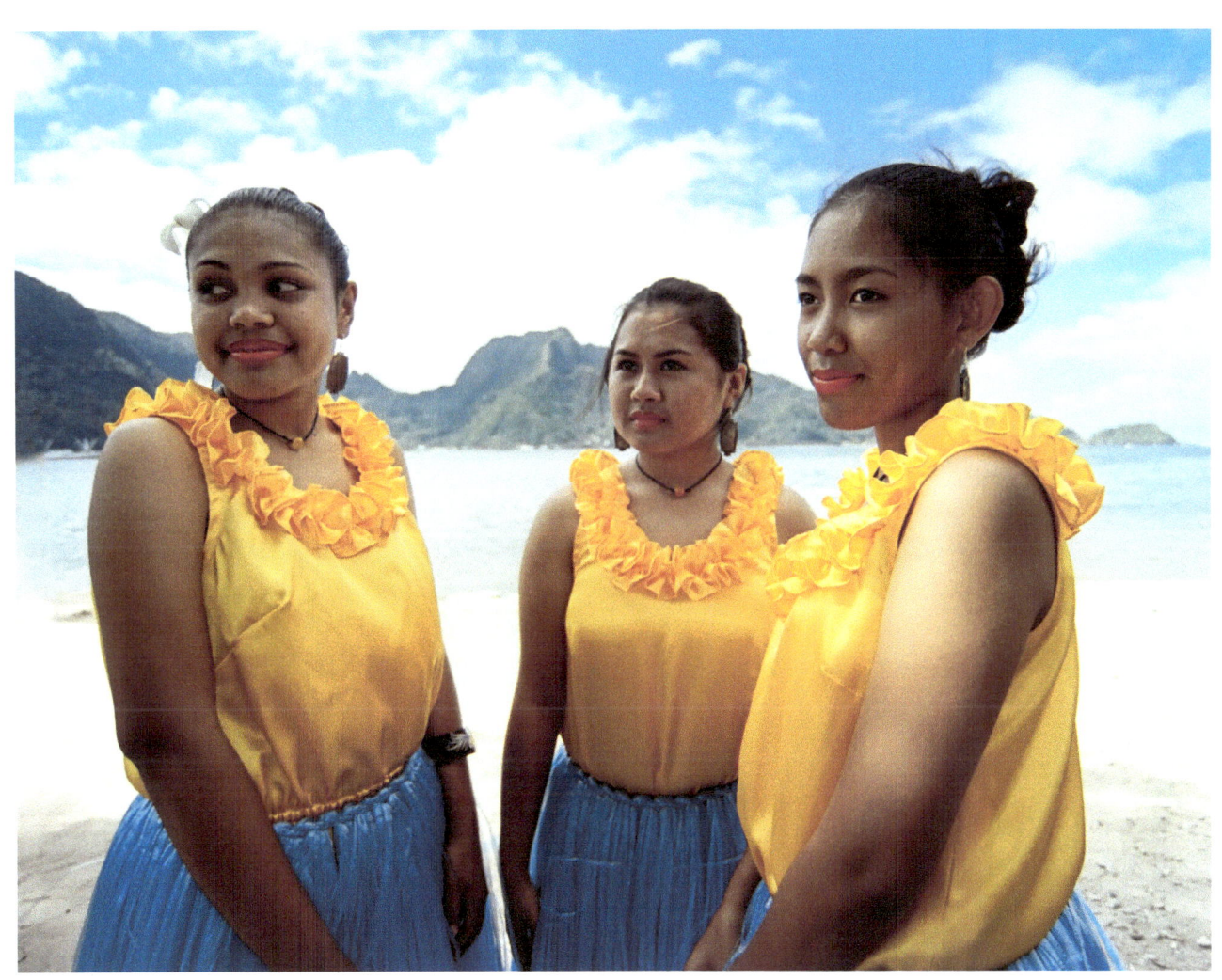

Dancers from Papua New Guinea.

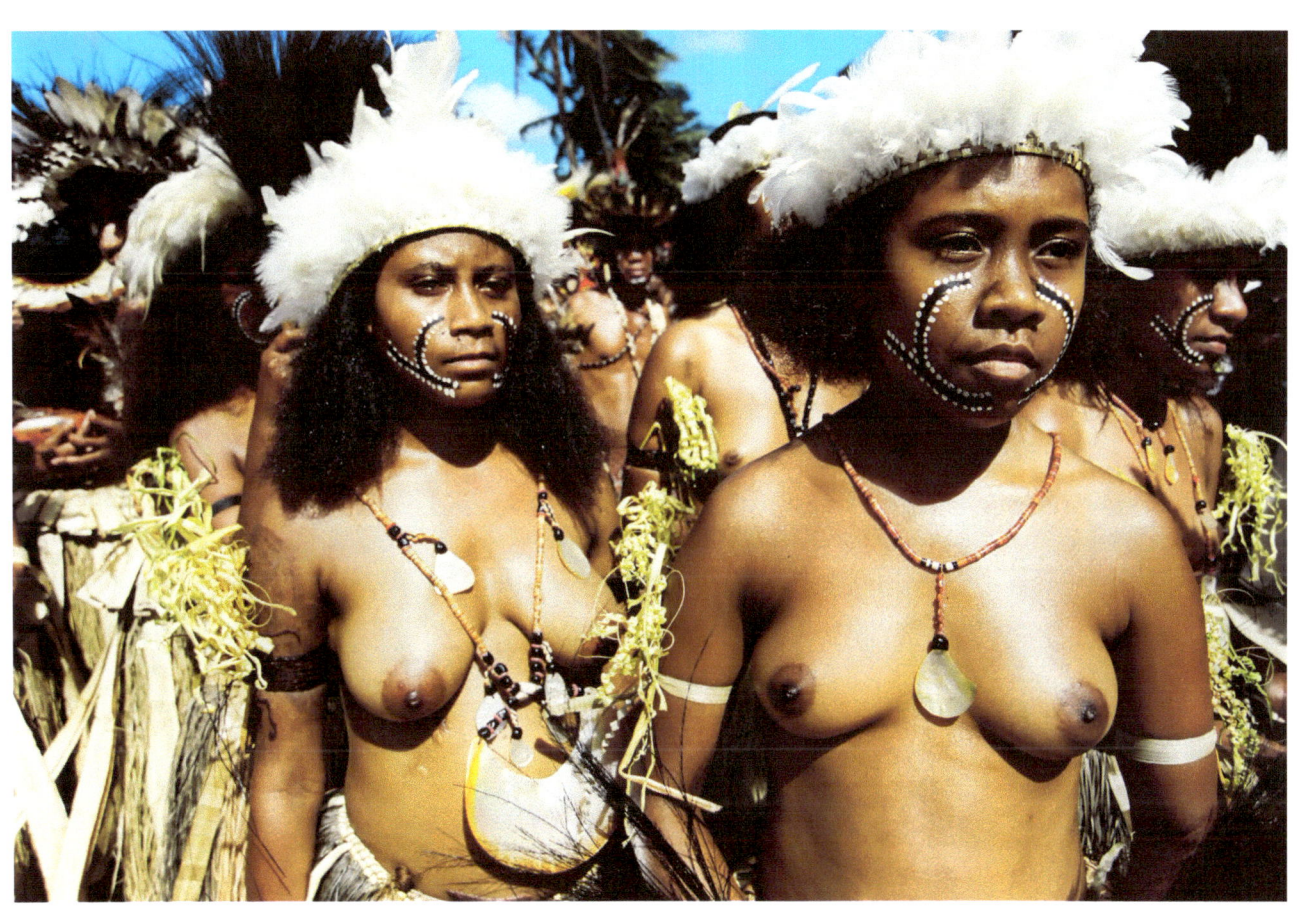

Two performers from Papua New Guinea at the malae of the Festival village.

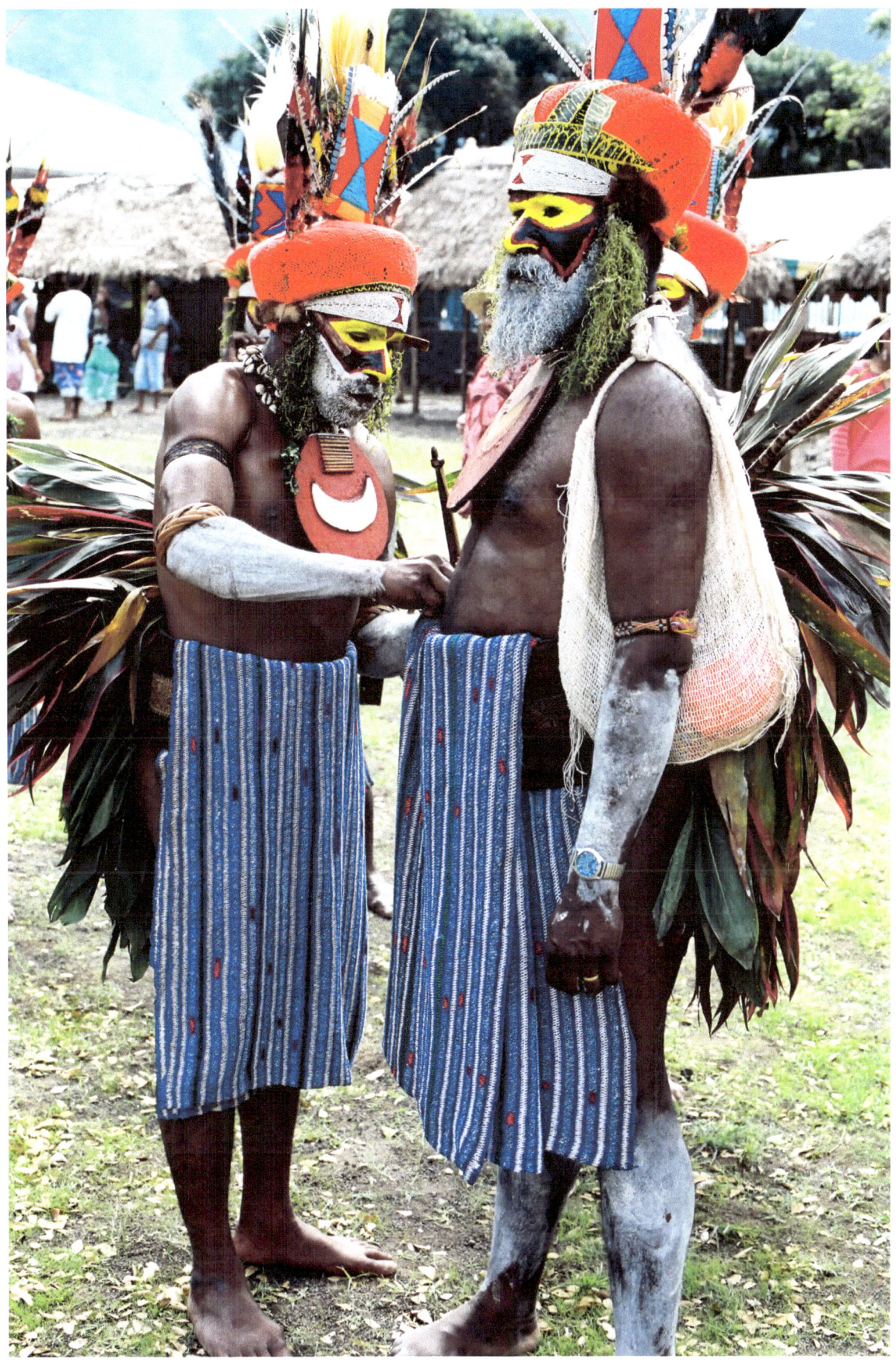

Performers from Papua New Guinea.

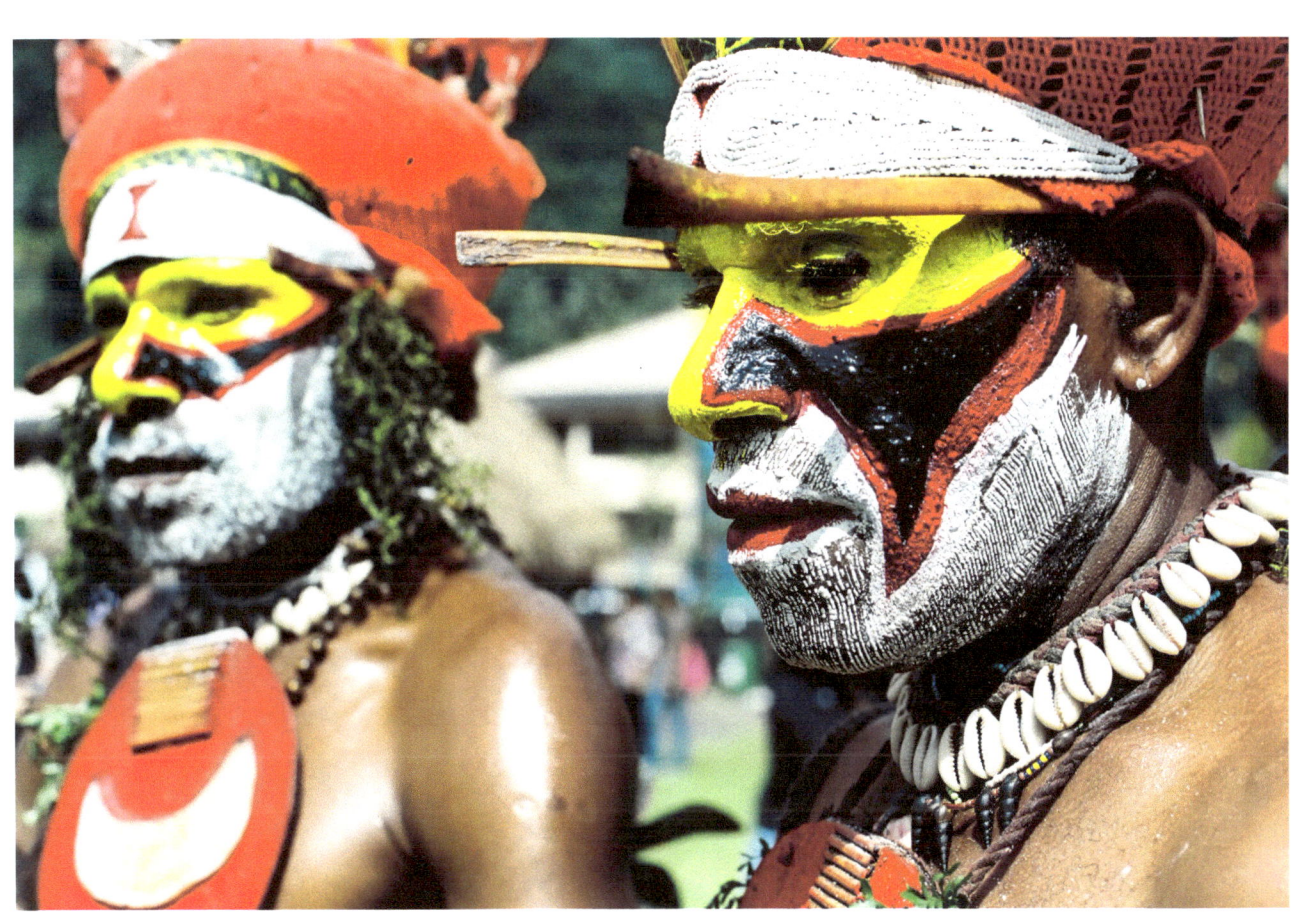

Three dancers from Papua New Guinea perform wearing hats made from woven human hair.

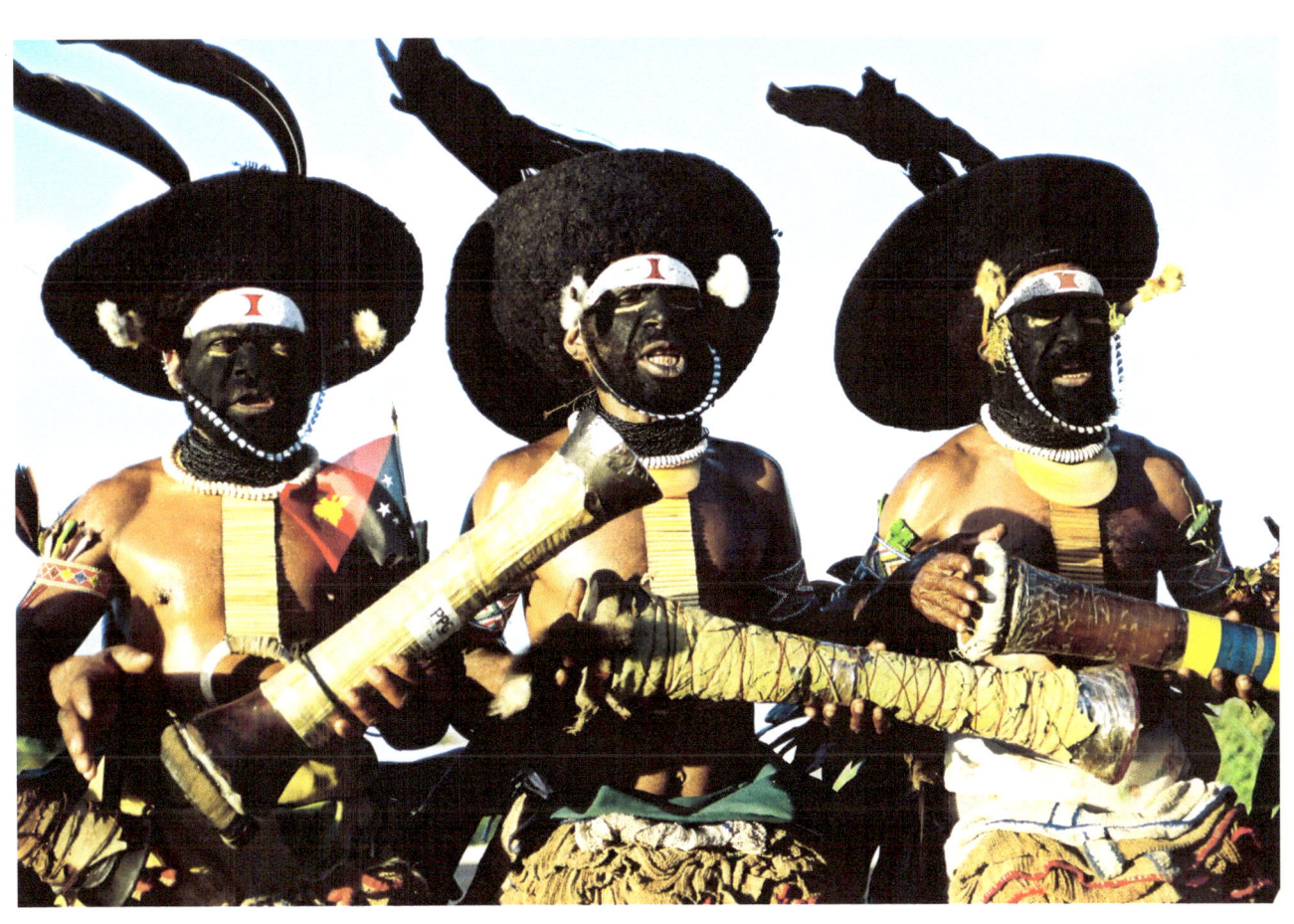

Members of the Rapa Nui (Easter Island) delegation.

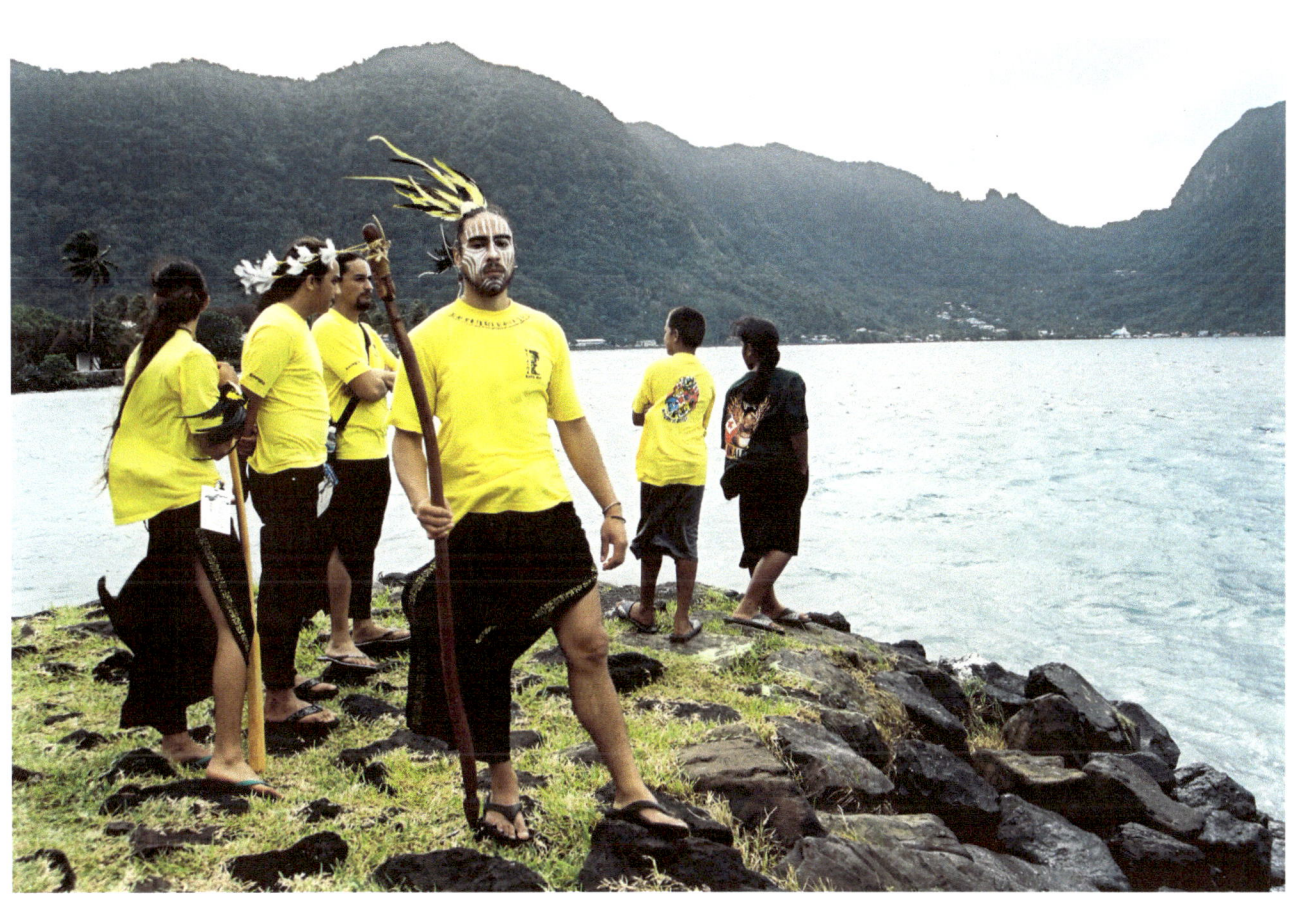

A Rapa Nui (Easter Island) dancer prepares his makeup using sunglasses as a mirror.

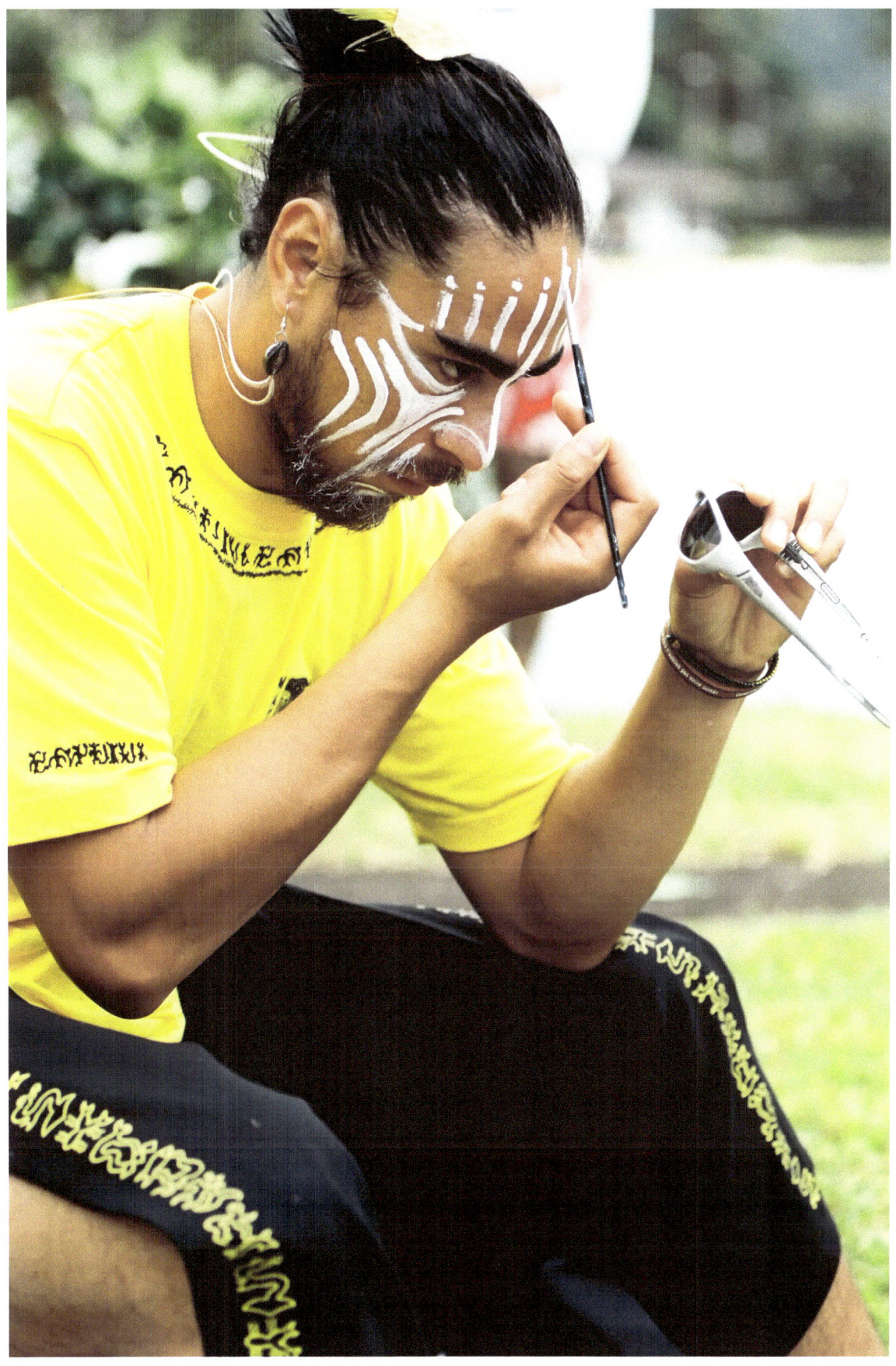

A performance by a dancer from Rapa Nui (Easter Island).

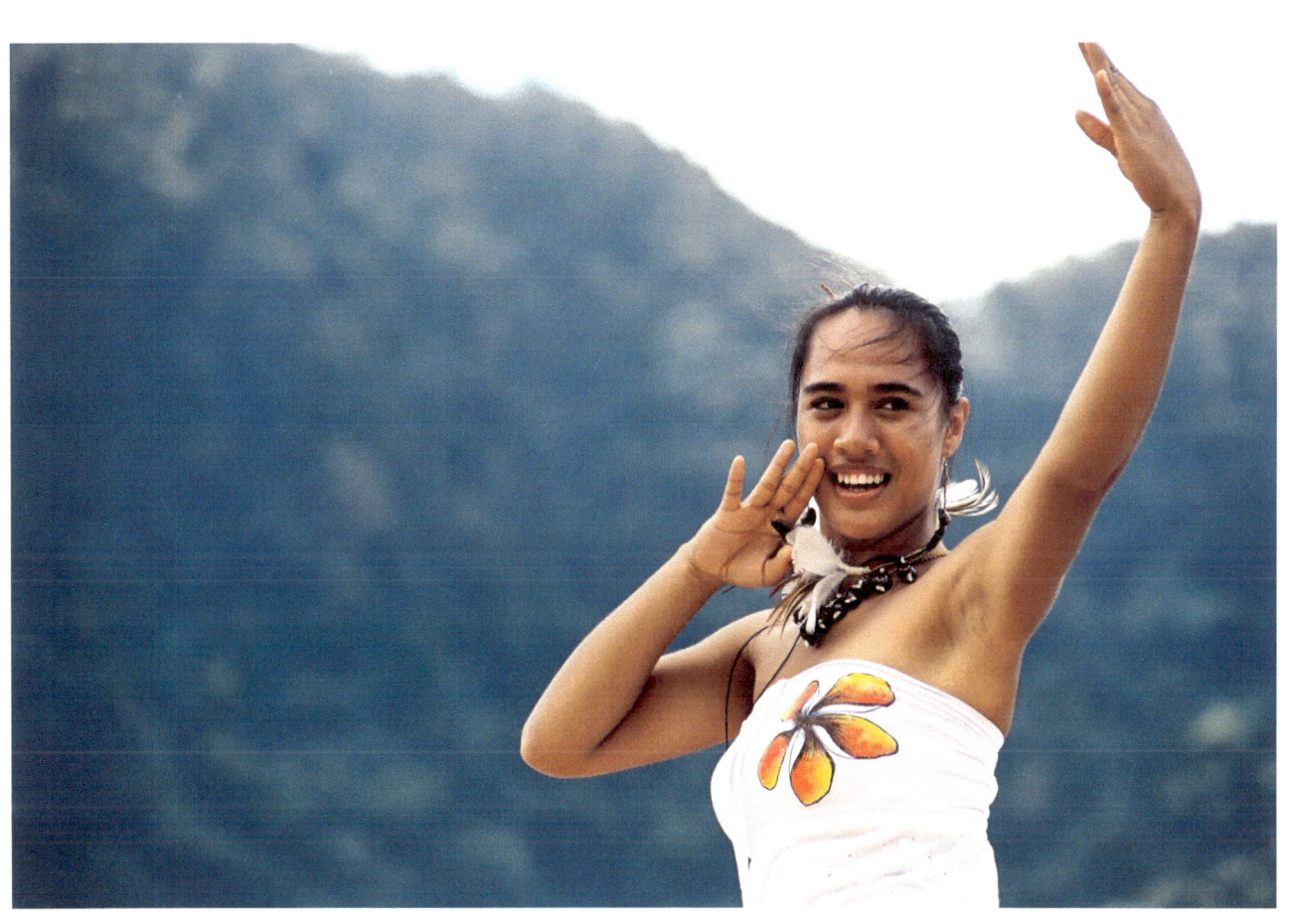

Rapa Nui (Easter Island) male dancers usually performed wearing body paint and loincloths.

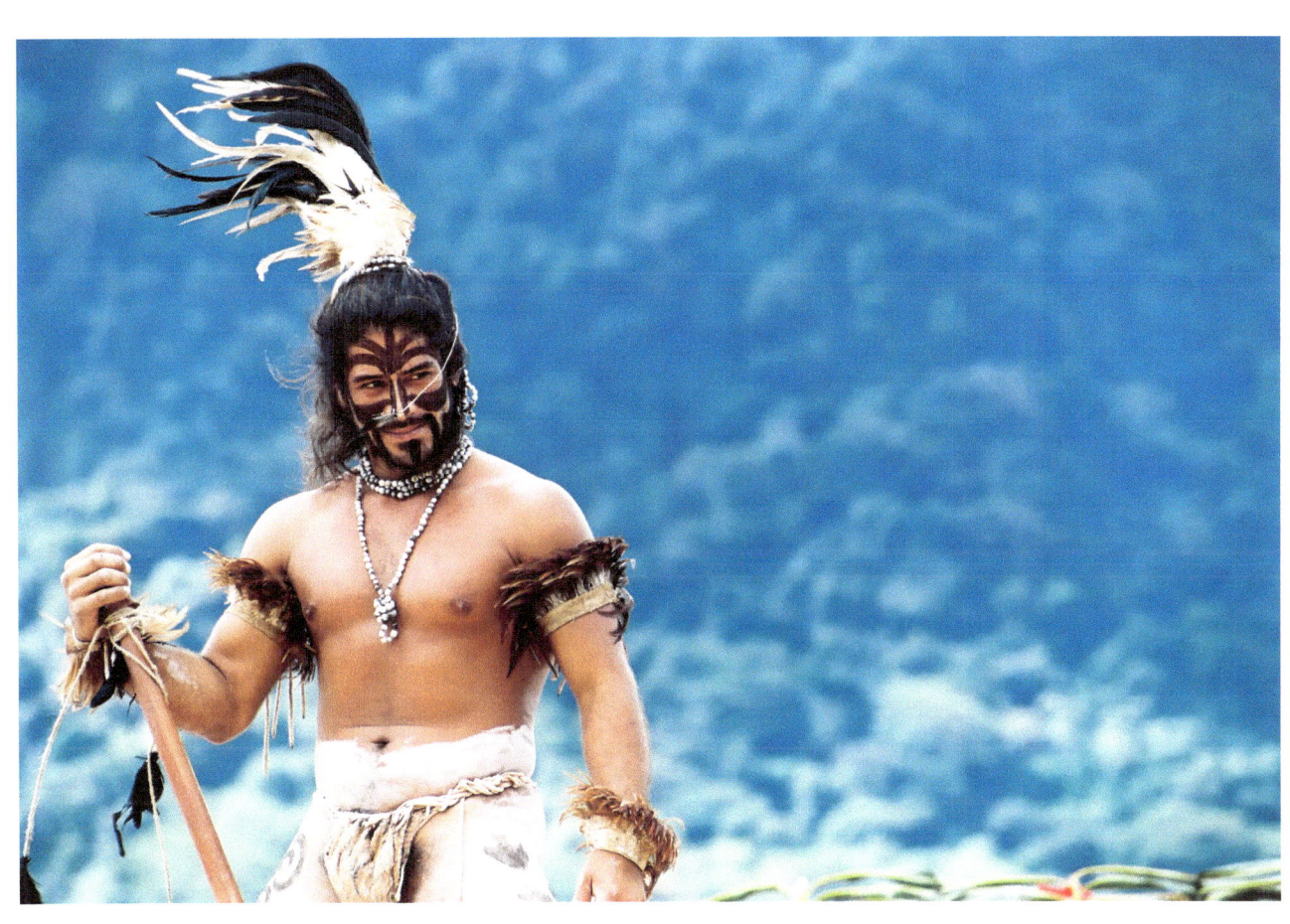

Dancers from Samoa.

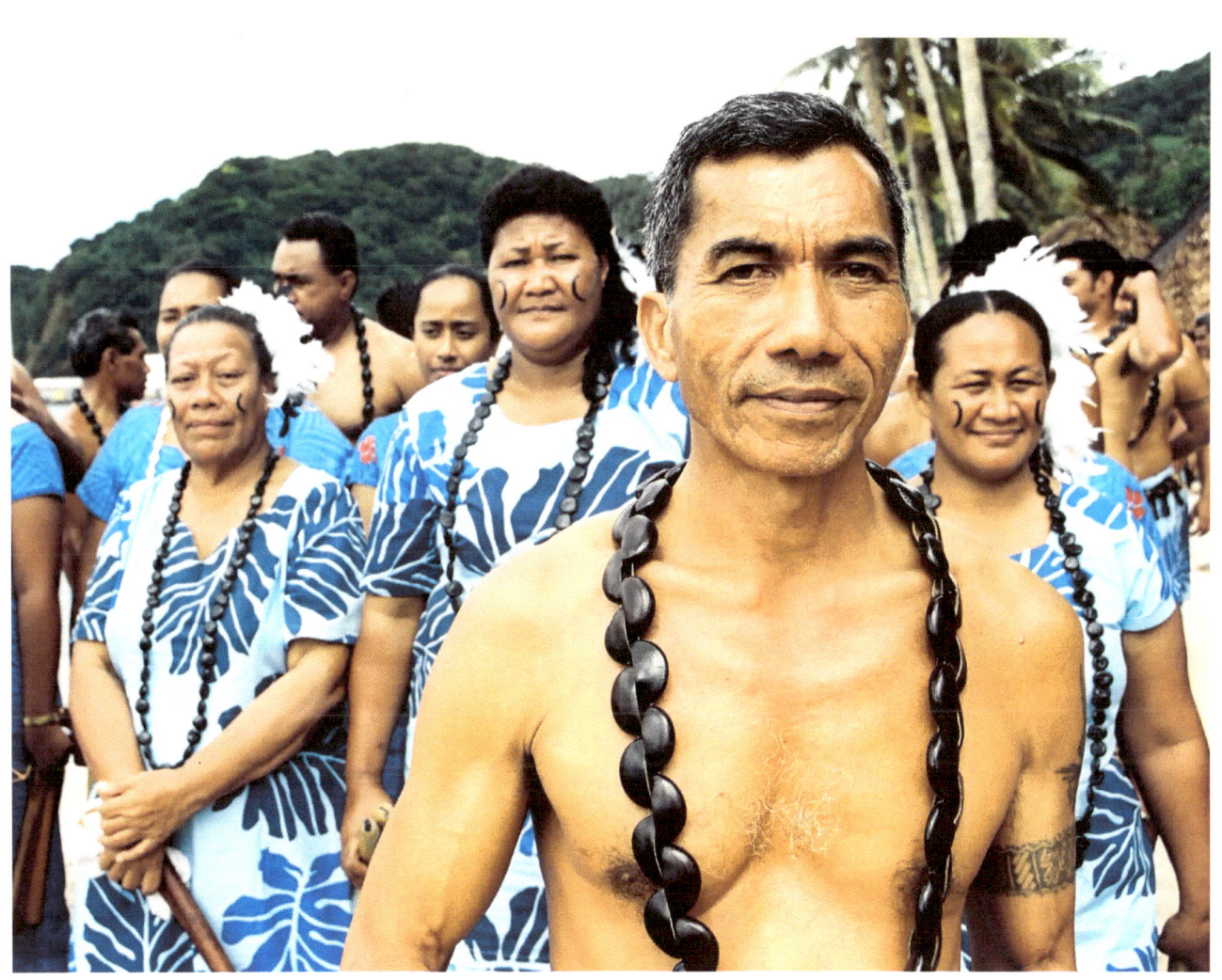

Dancers from the large Samoa delegation were a crowd favorite at the Festival.

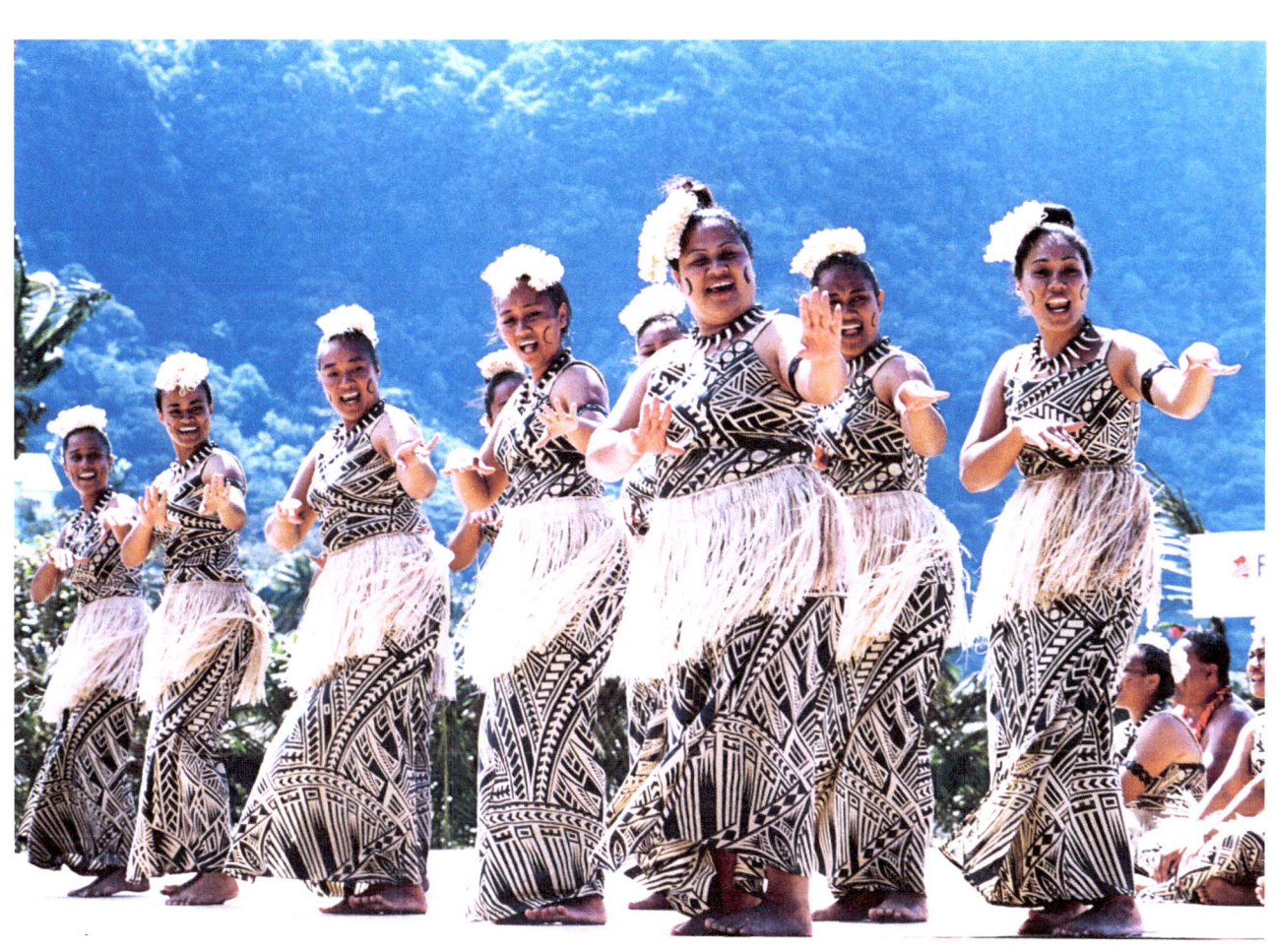

A young performer from Samoa sports two contemporary tattoos.

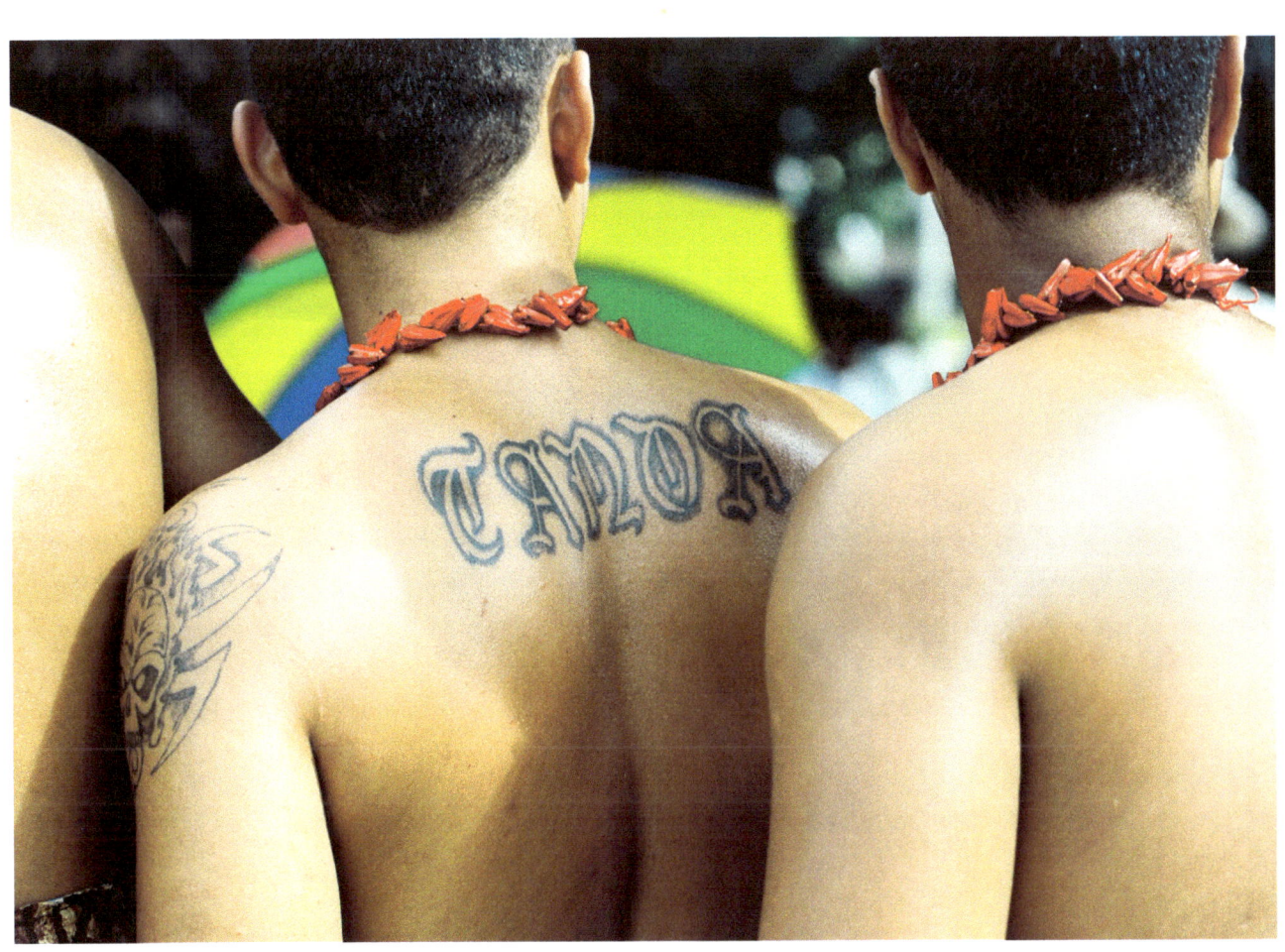

Two performers from Samoa, with their traditional men's tattoo called the pe'a visible, watch another group.

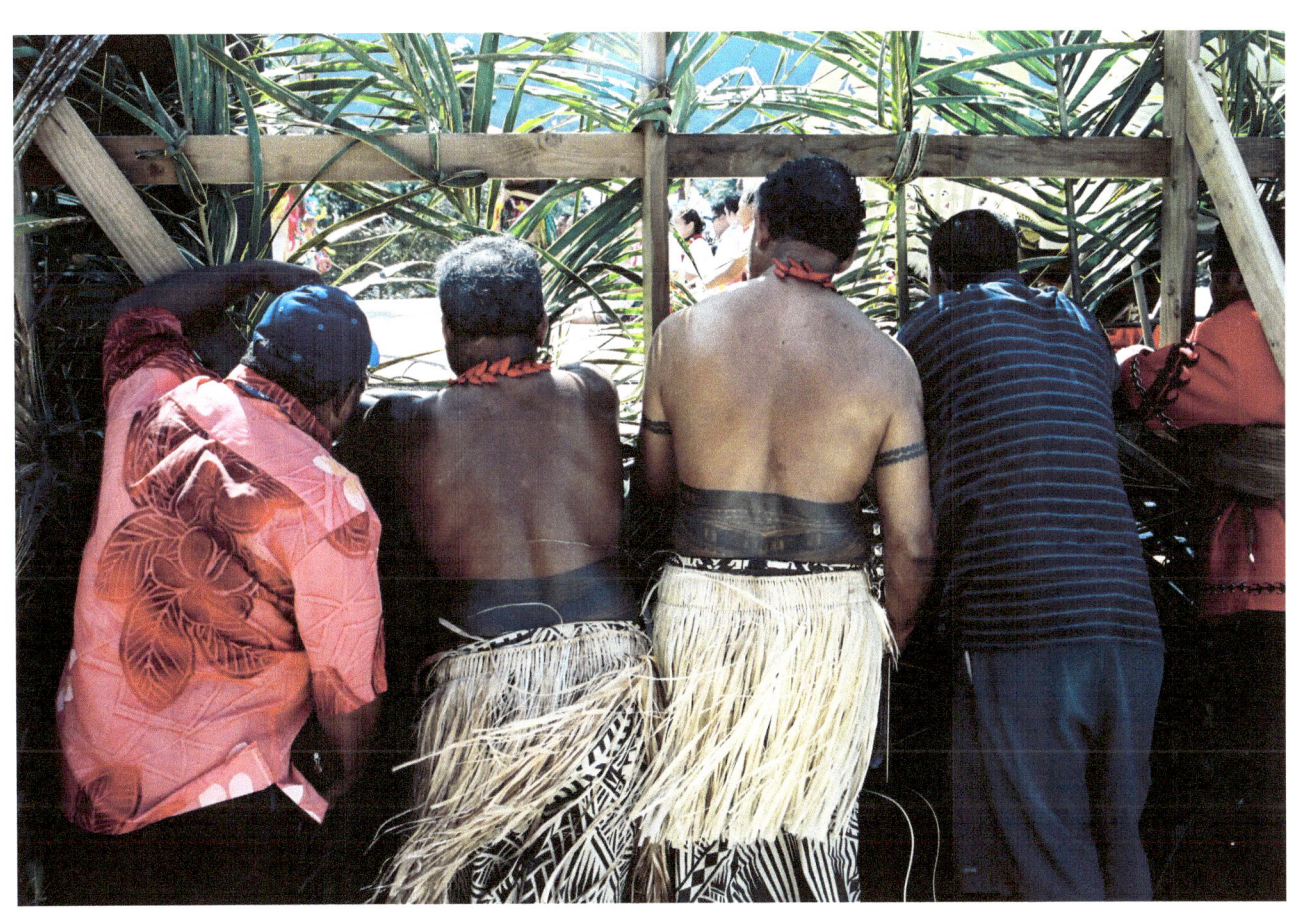

Performers from Samoa dance on the Utulei Beach stage.

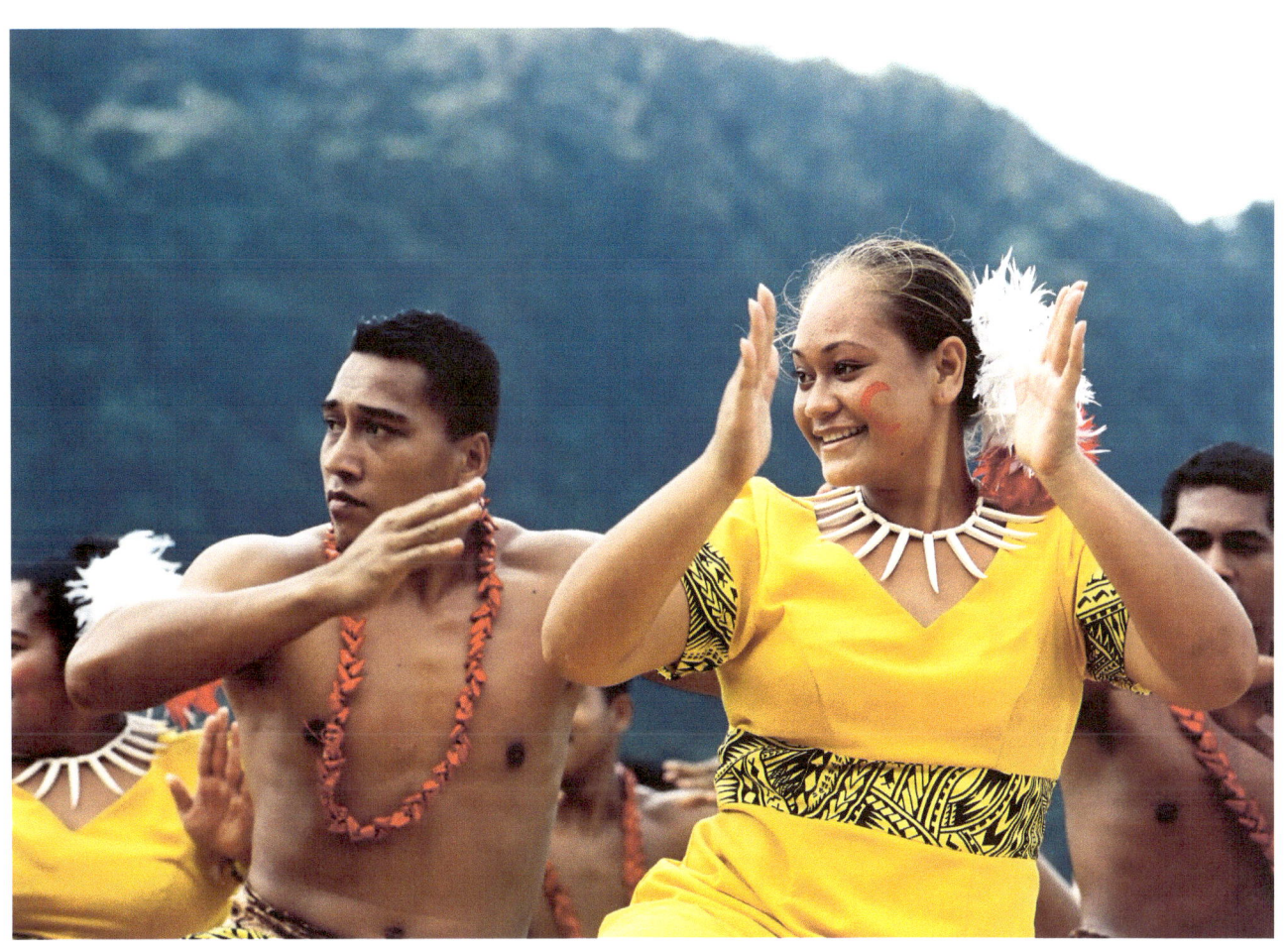

Solomon Island dancers, wearing their traditional attire, prepare to take a bamboo percussion instrument on stage.

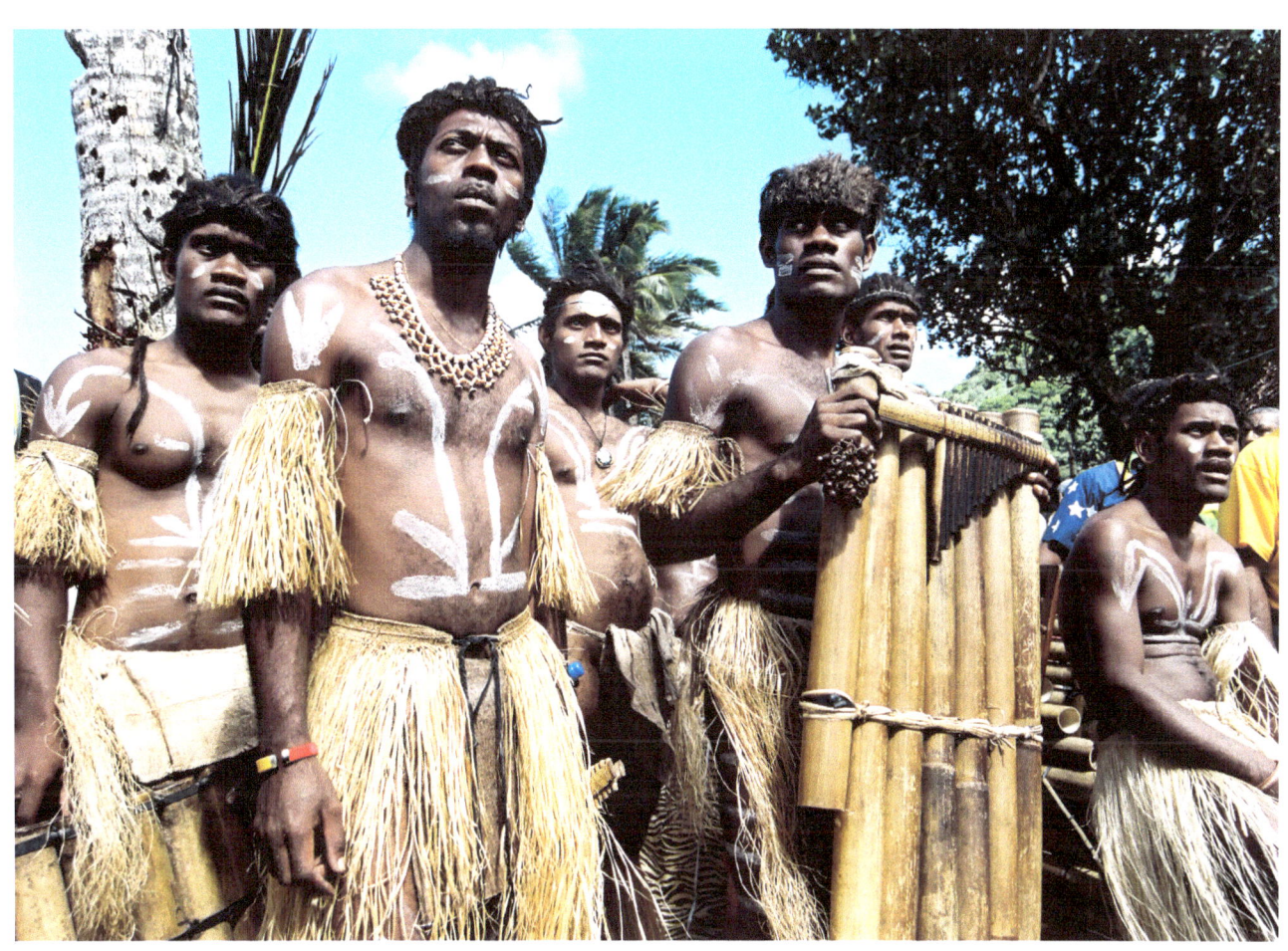

Three Solomon Island performers play traditional panpipes, while a fourth plays a bamboo percussion instrument.

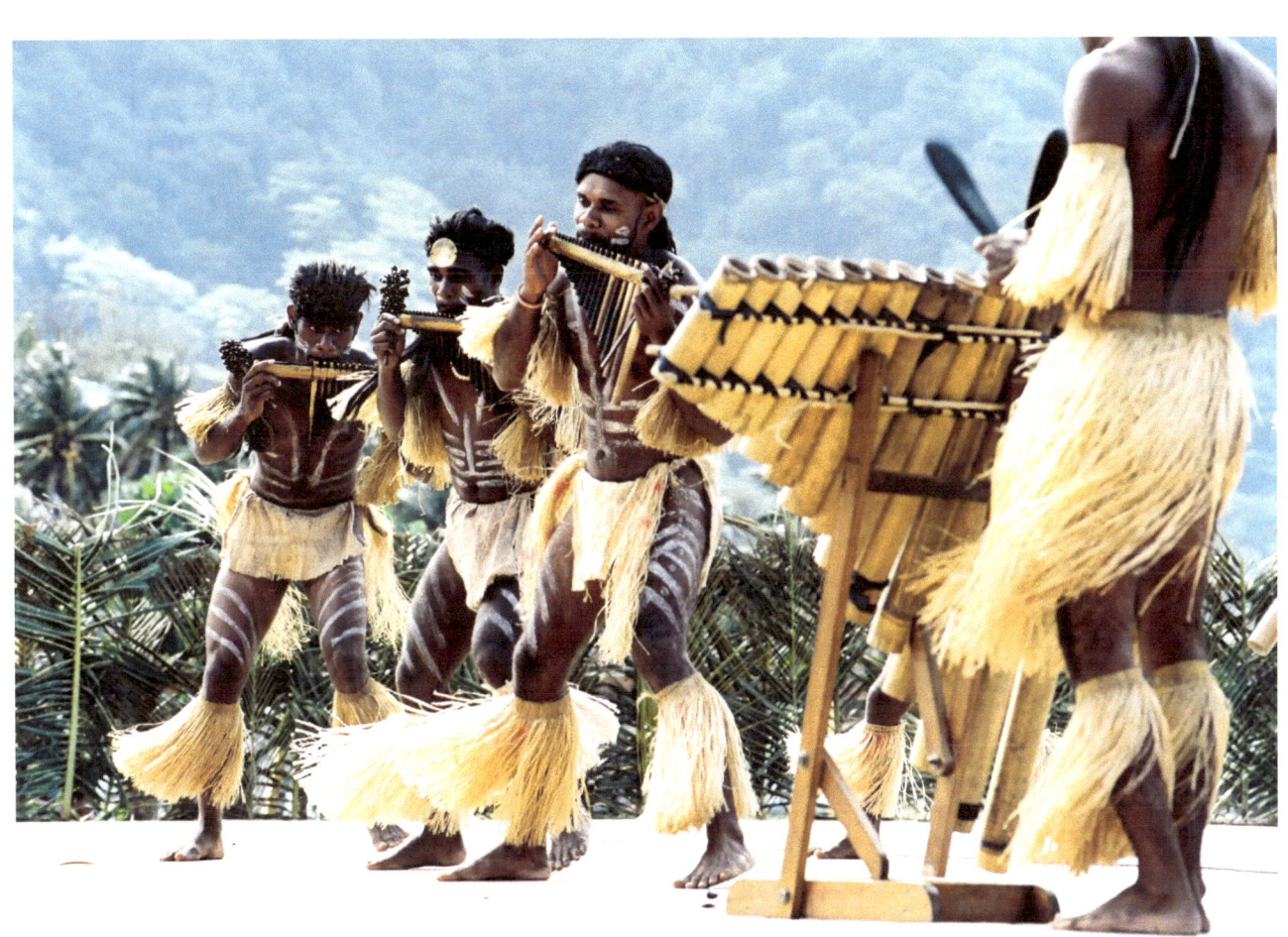

One of the leading male performers with the popular Tahiti group watches
another troupe perform.

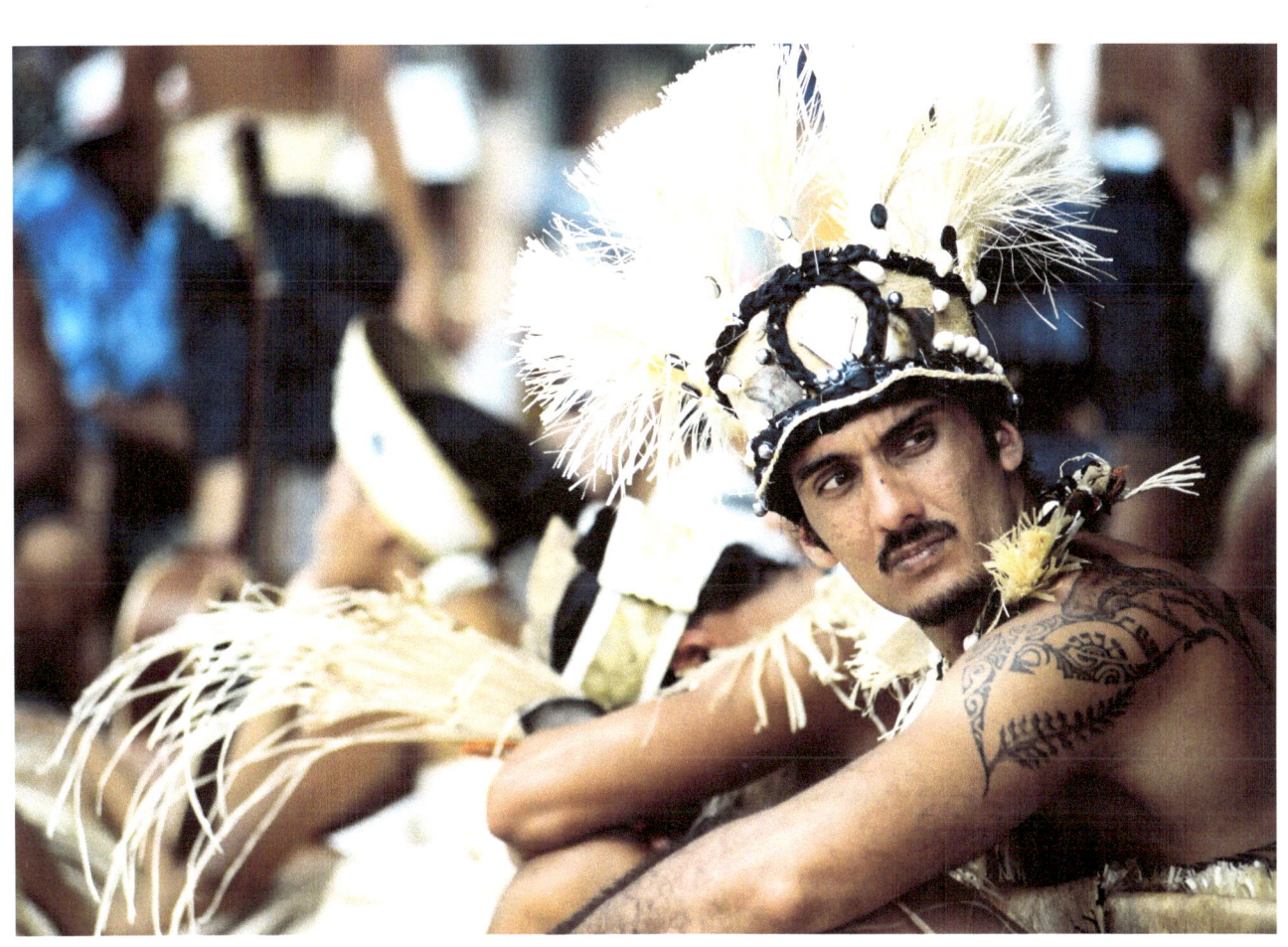

A dancer with the large Tahiti delegation.

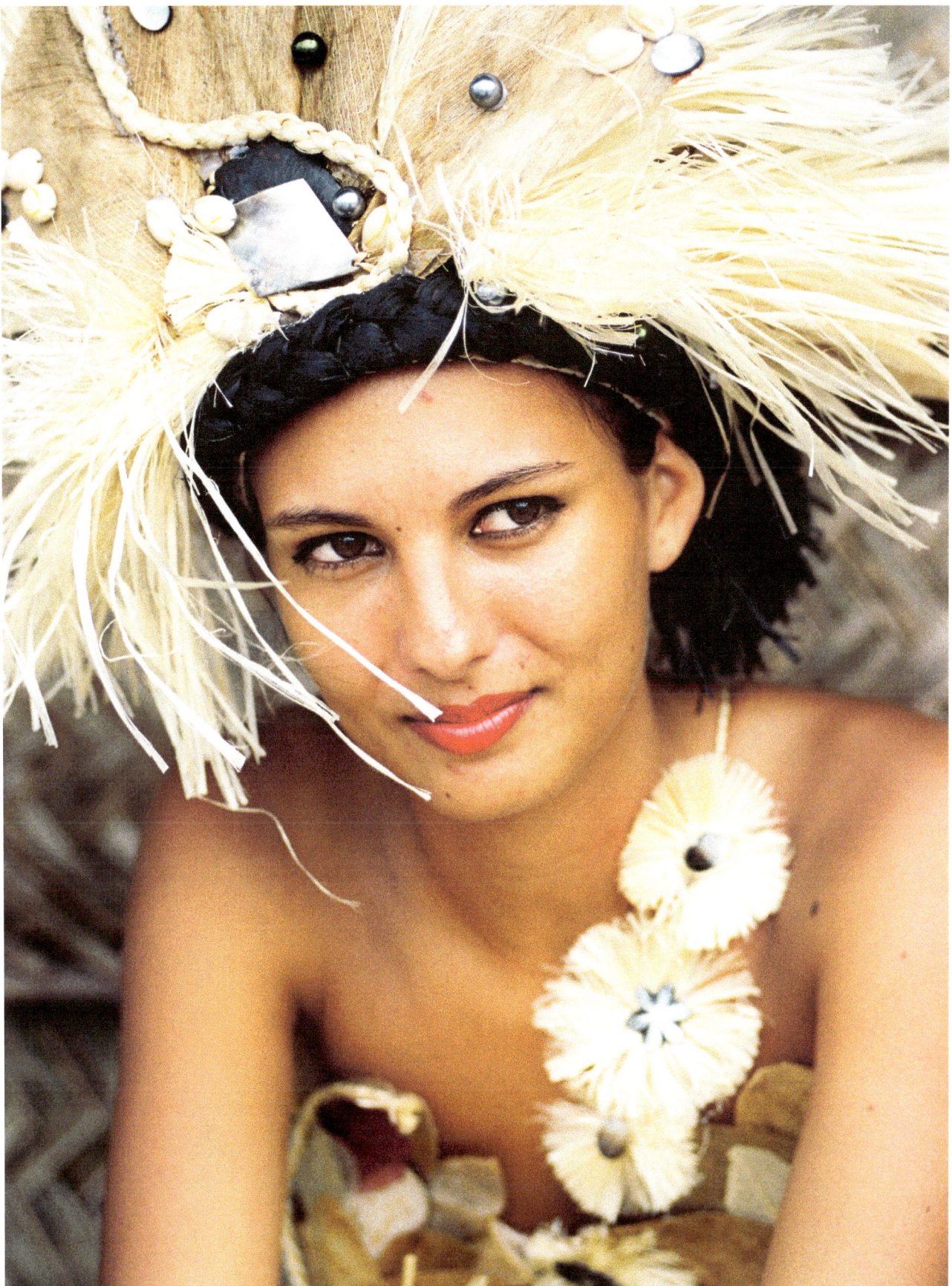

Members of the Tahiti troupe pray before going on stage.

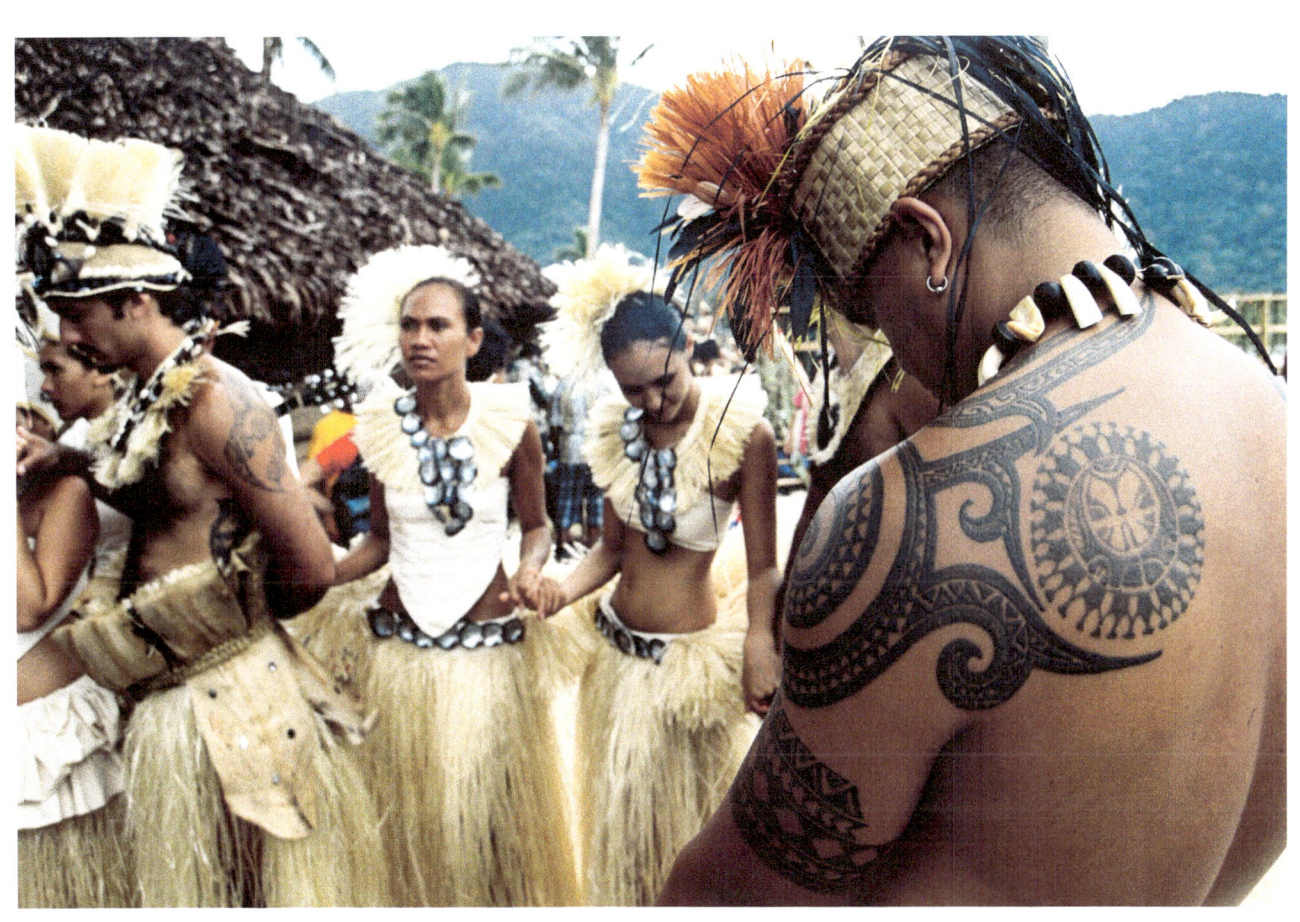

The Tahitian dancers were among the most polished and popular performers at the Festival.

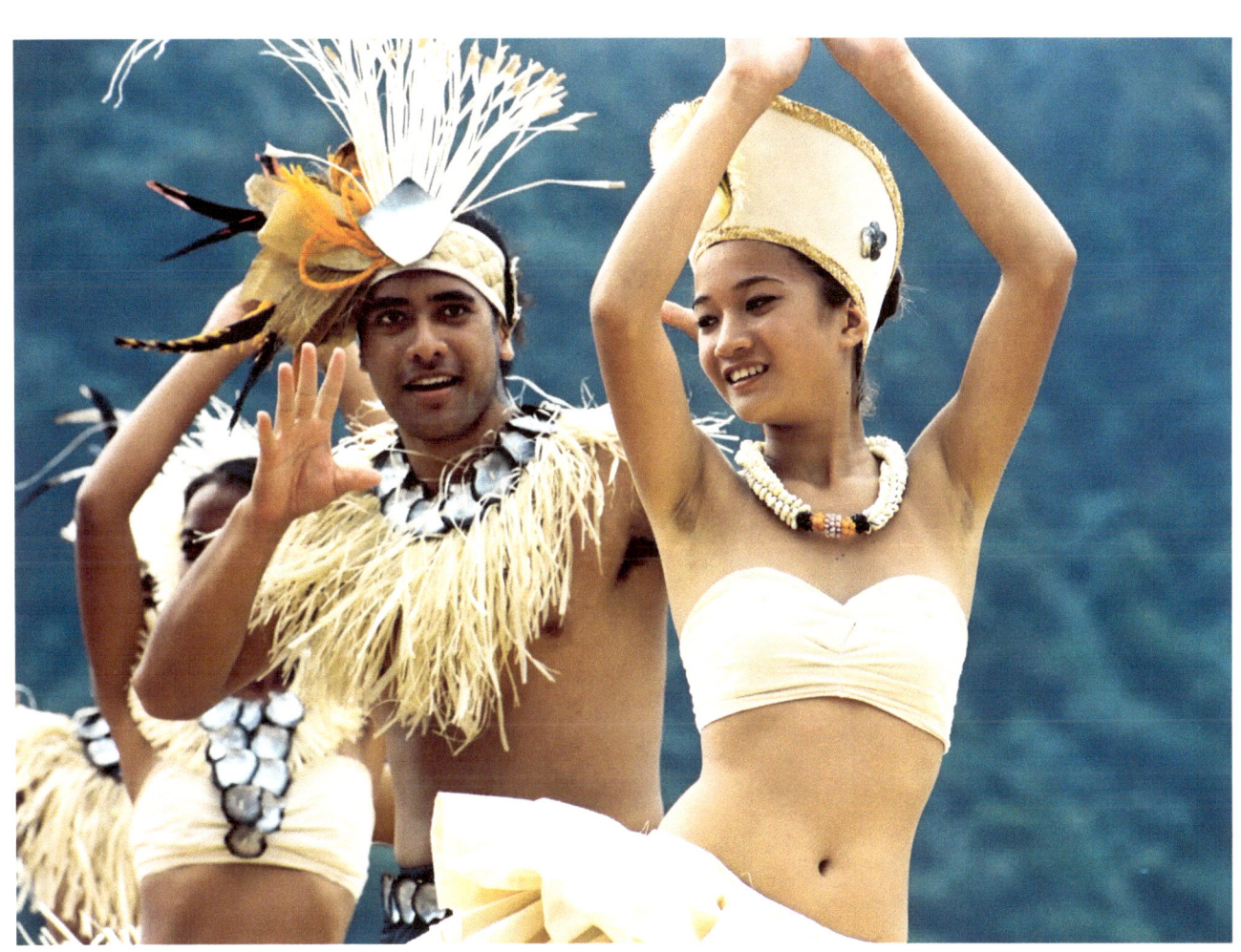

Four females from the Tahiti group pose with male dancers from New Caledonia.

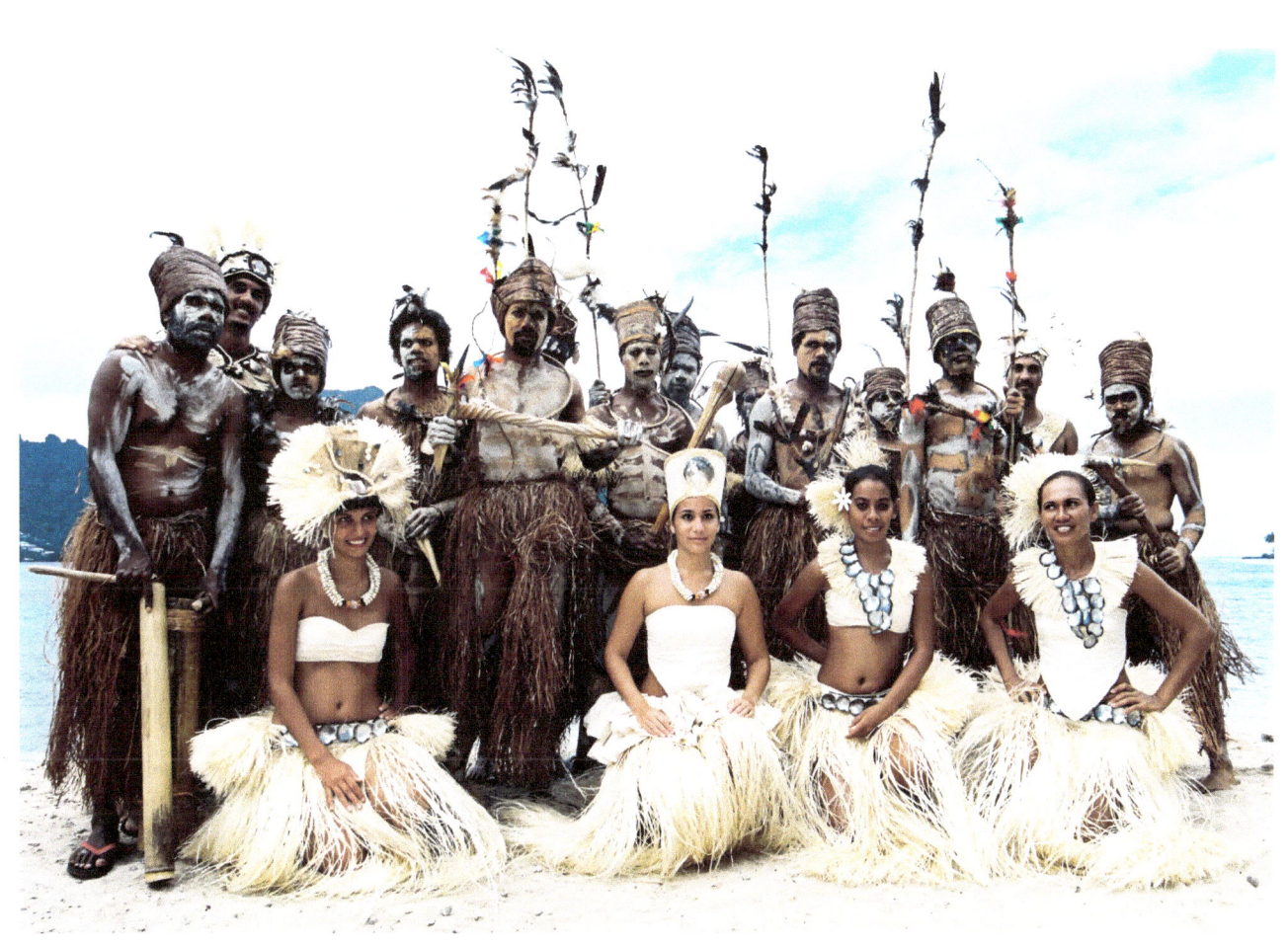

The male dancers from Tahiti performed with a physical style that was popular with women in the audience.

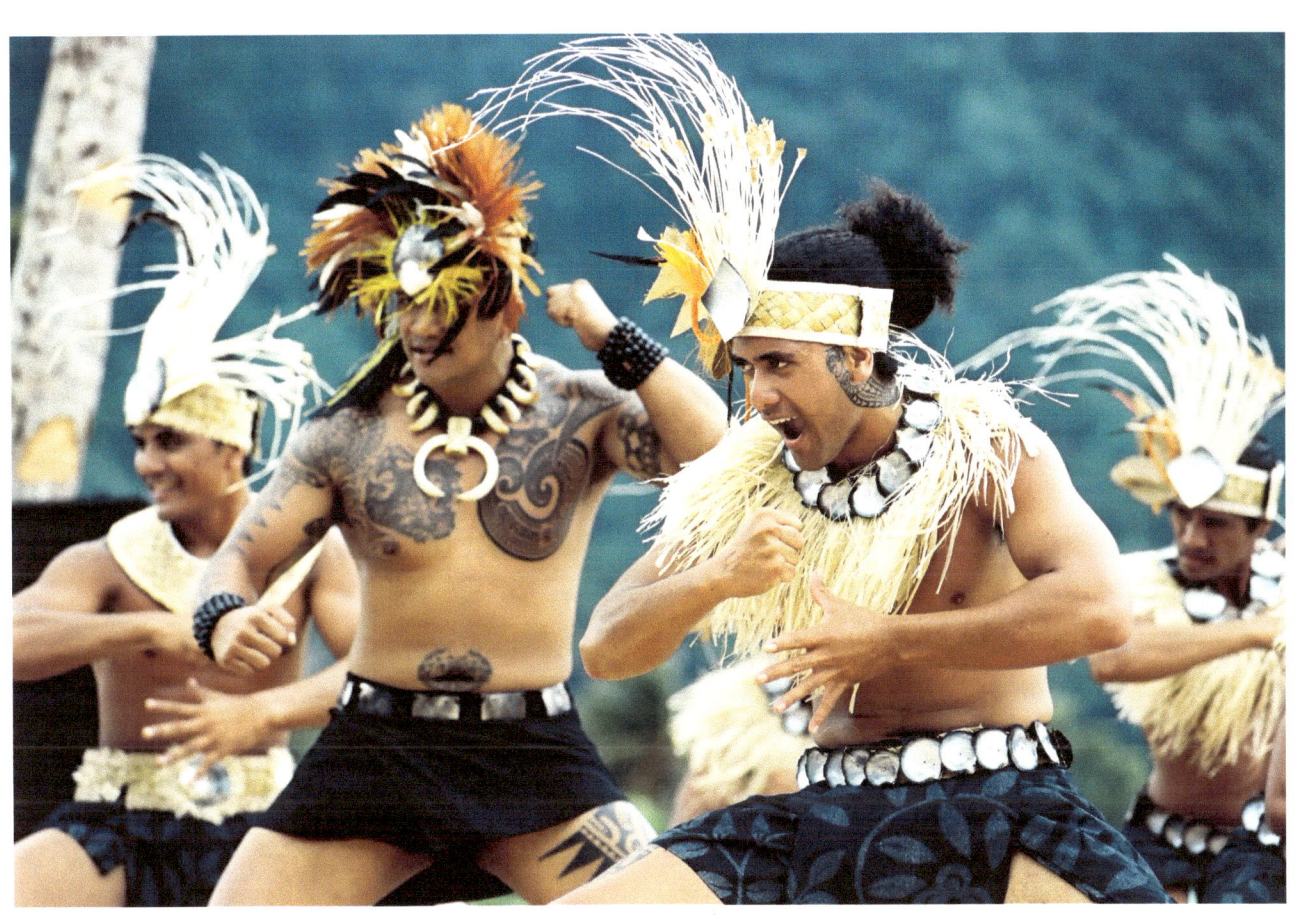

Two members of the aboriginal group from Taiwan hold an impromptu performance. There is evidence that some Pacific Islanders trace their ancestry to the aboriginal population of Taiwan.

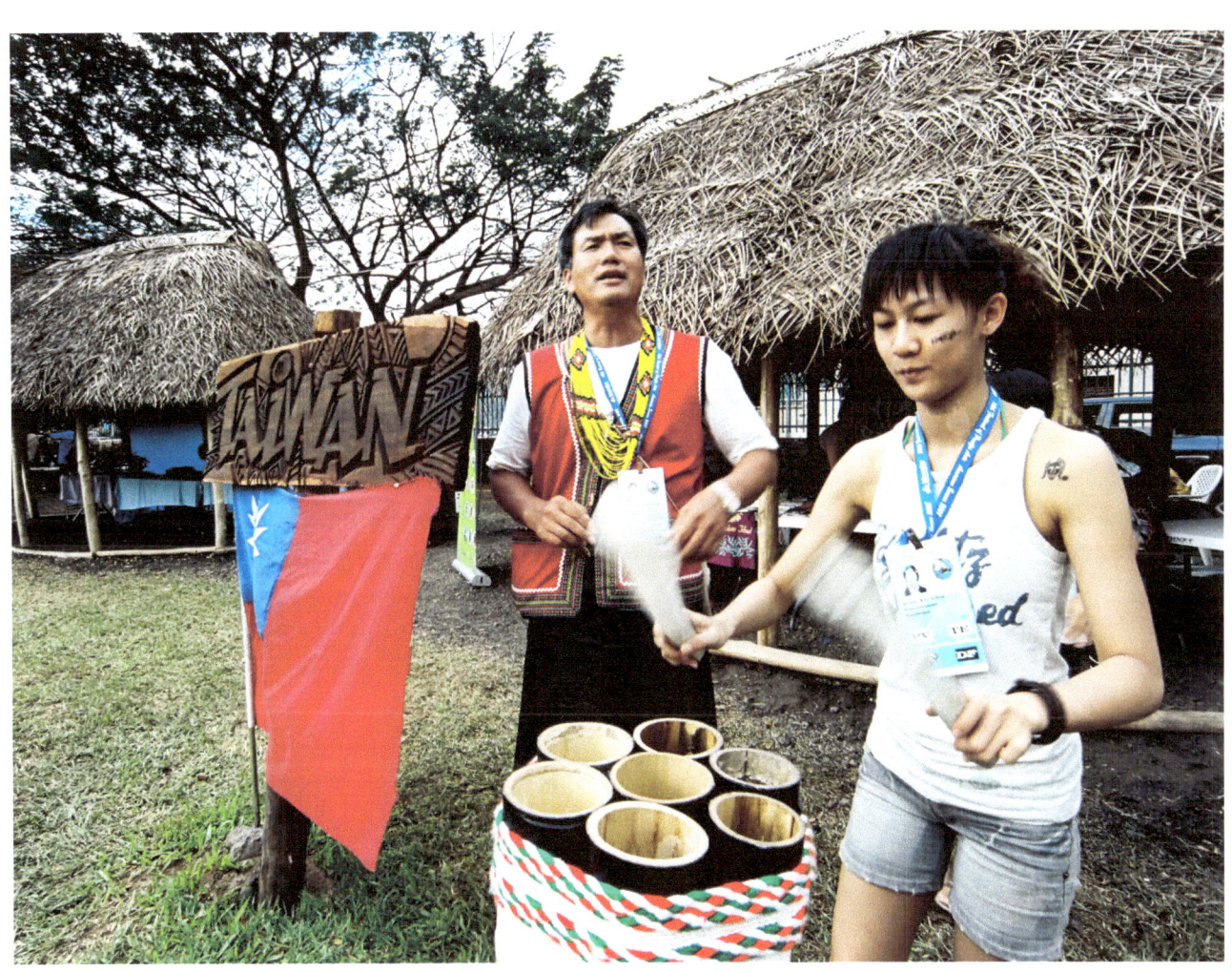

Four performers from the Taiwan aboriginal group.

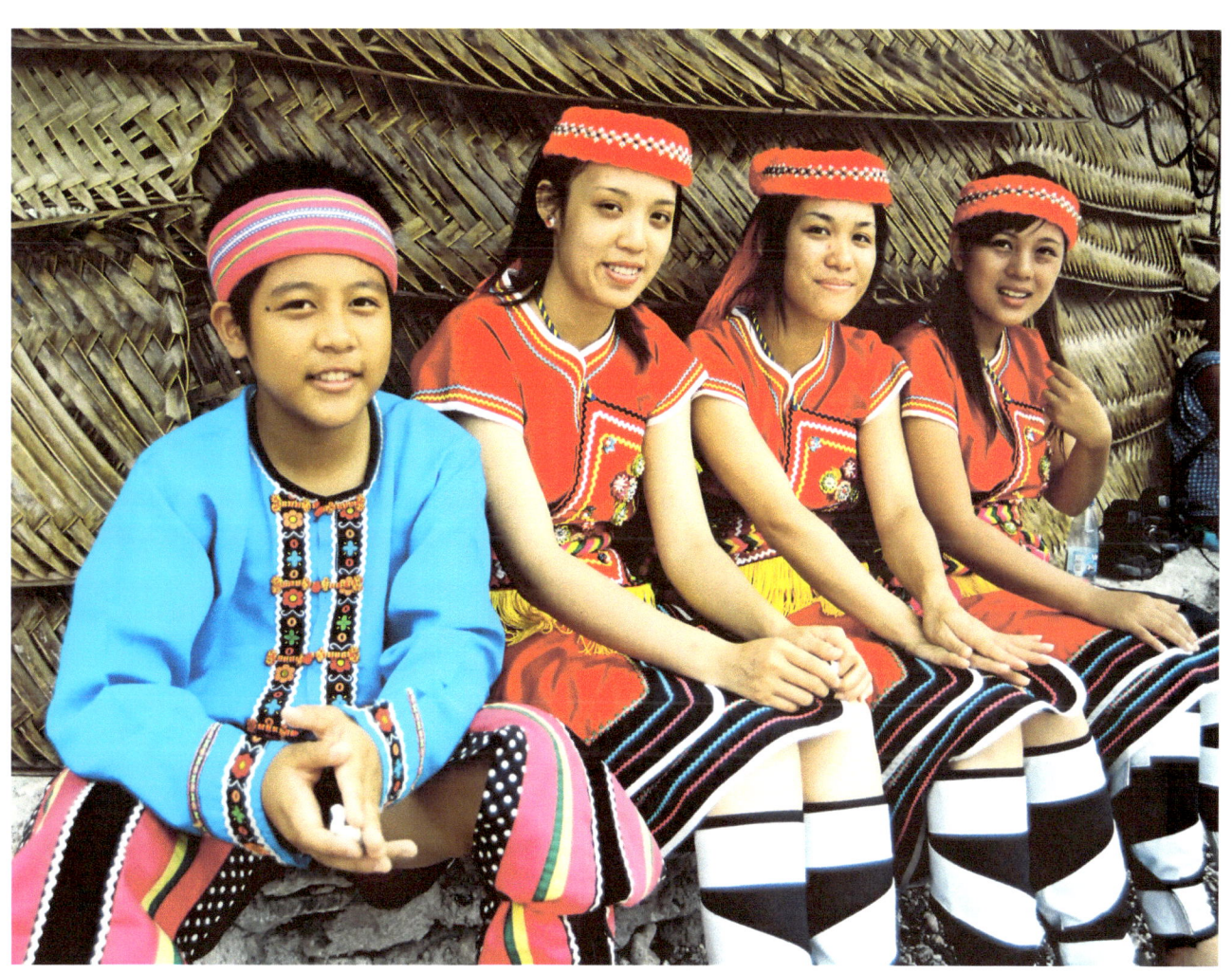

Dancers from Tokelau, a New Zealand protectorate near Samoa.

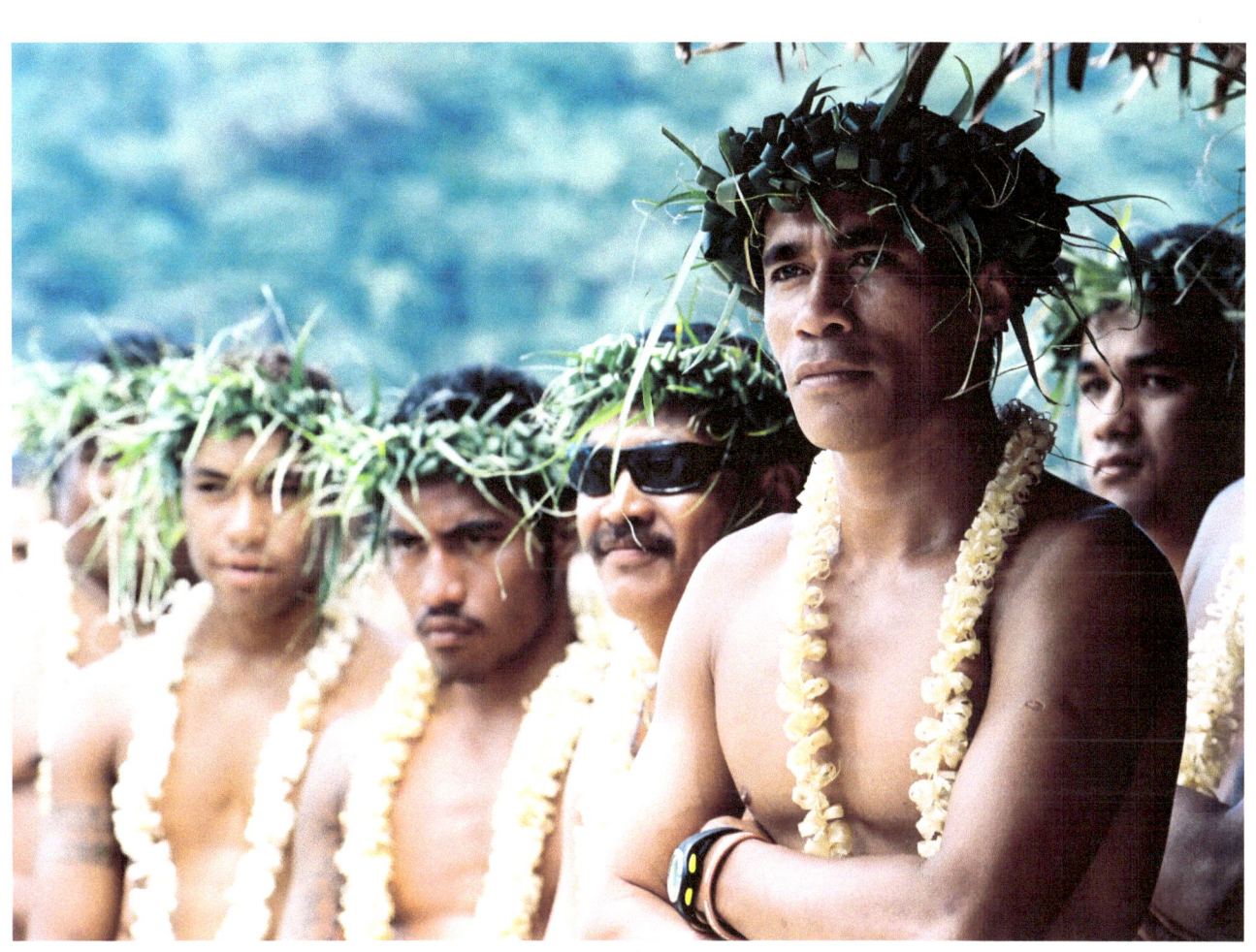

The Tokelau troupe dance and sing on the stage at Utulei Beach.

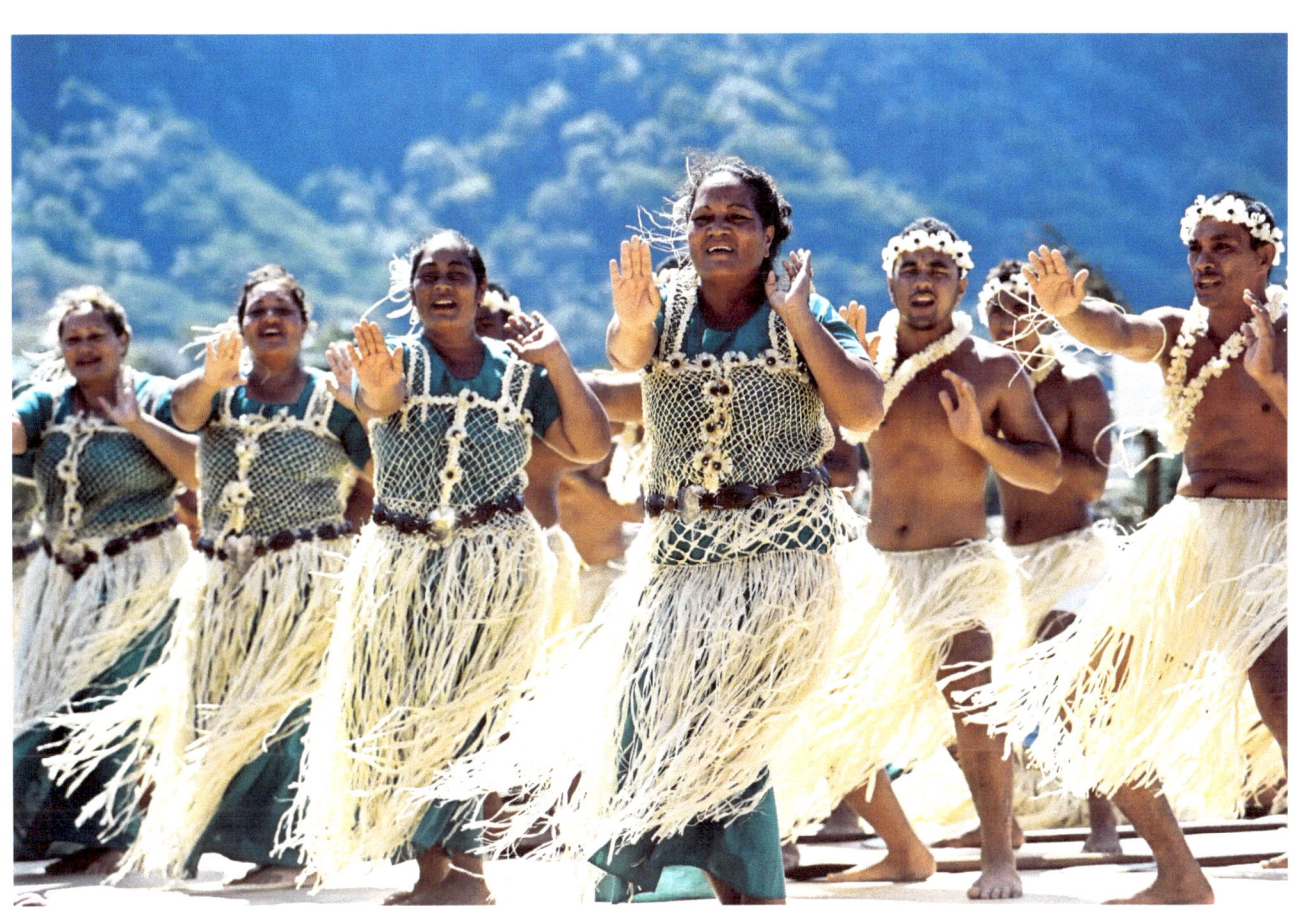

A member of Tonga's large delegation performs a solo dance.

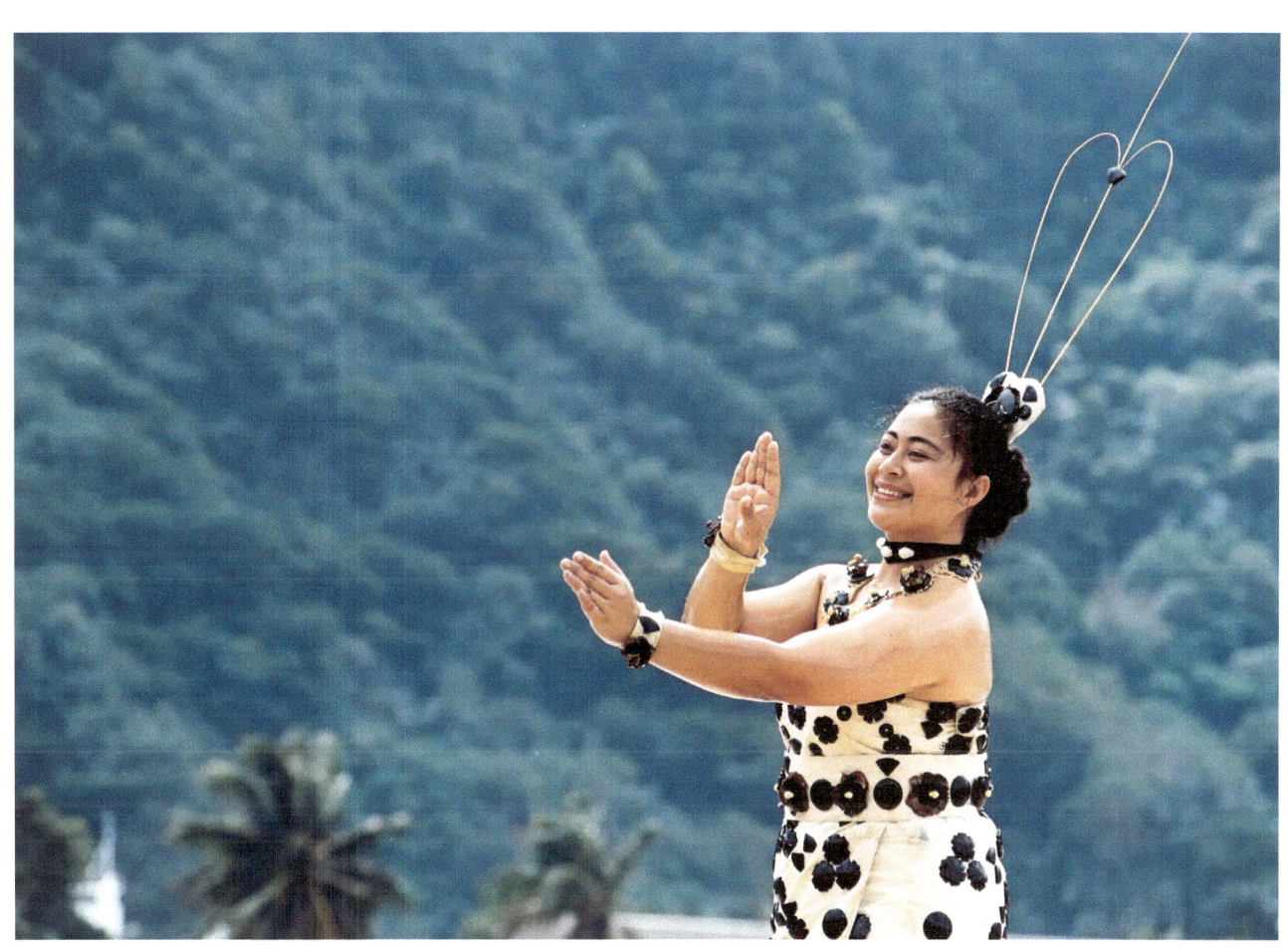

Tonga's group included a modern dance troupe that blended traditional and contemporary moves.

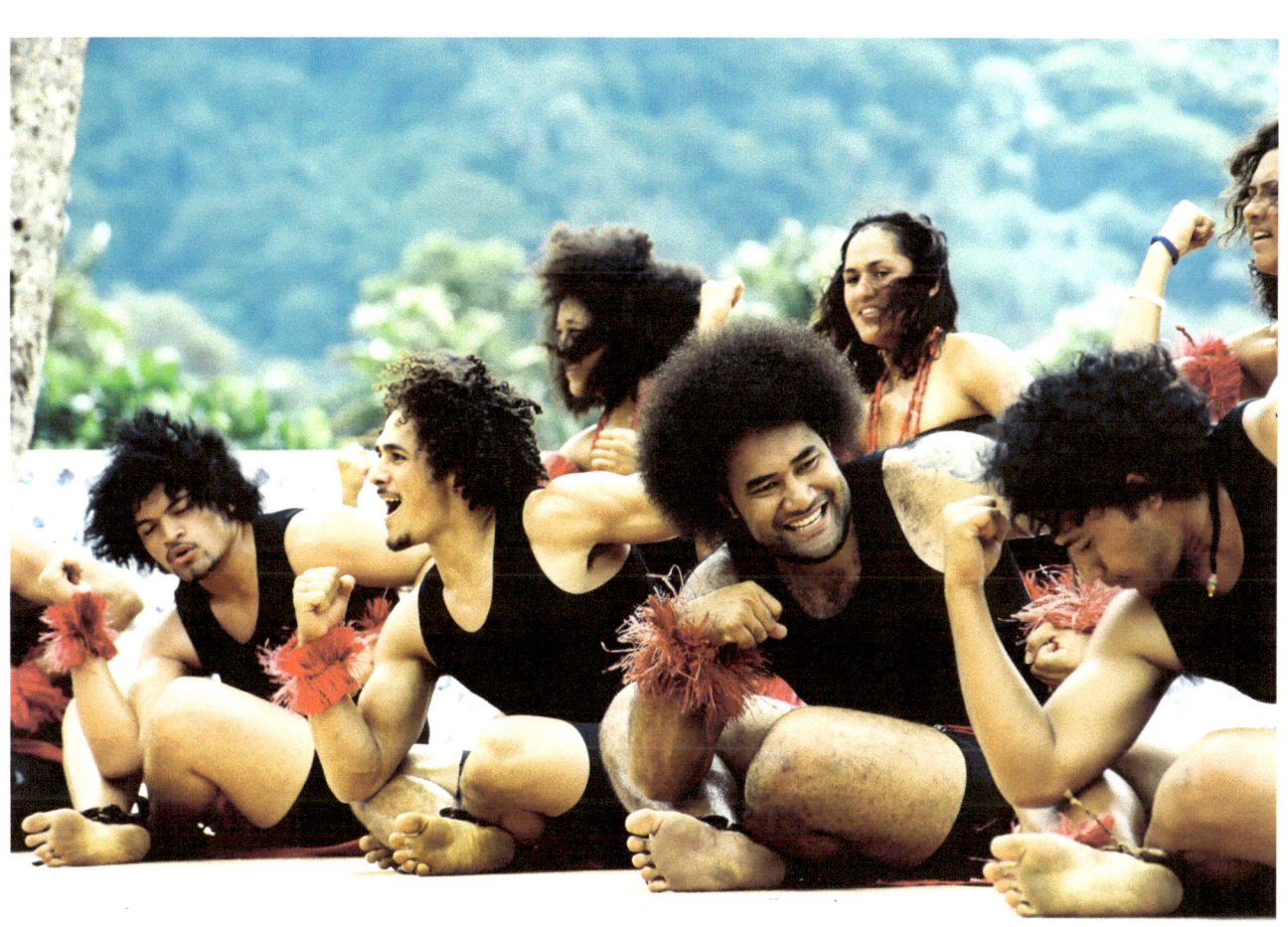

A dancer from Tonga sports a tattoo of the national seal on his back.

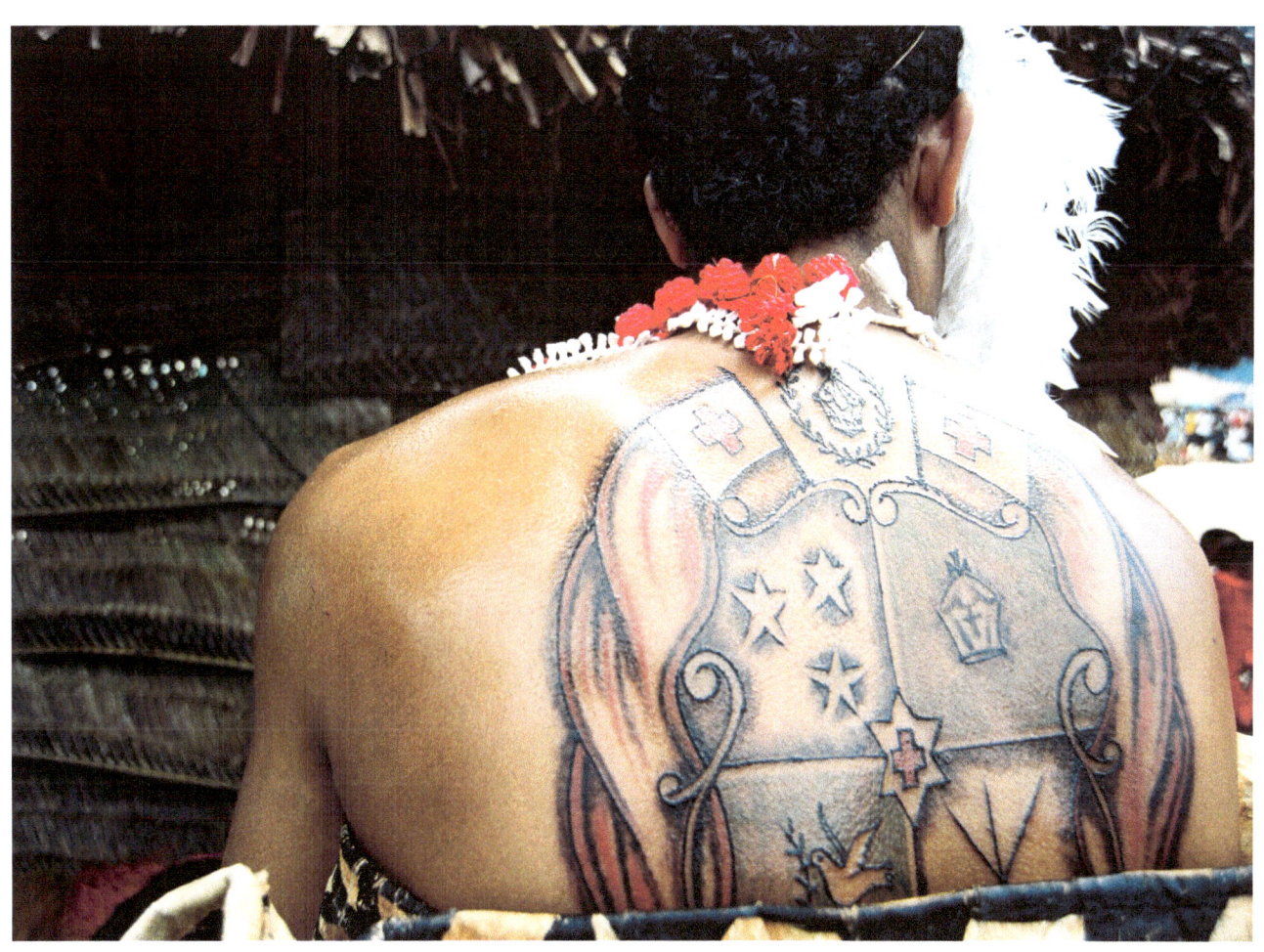

Tongans wear different interpretations of the ta'ovala around their waists.

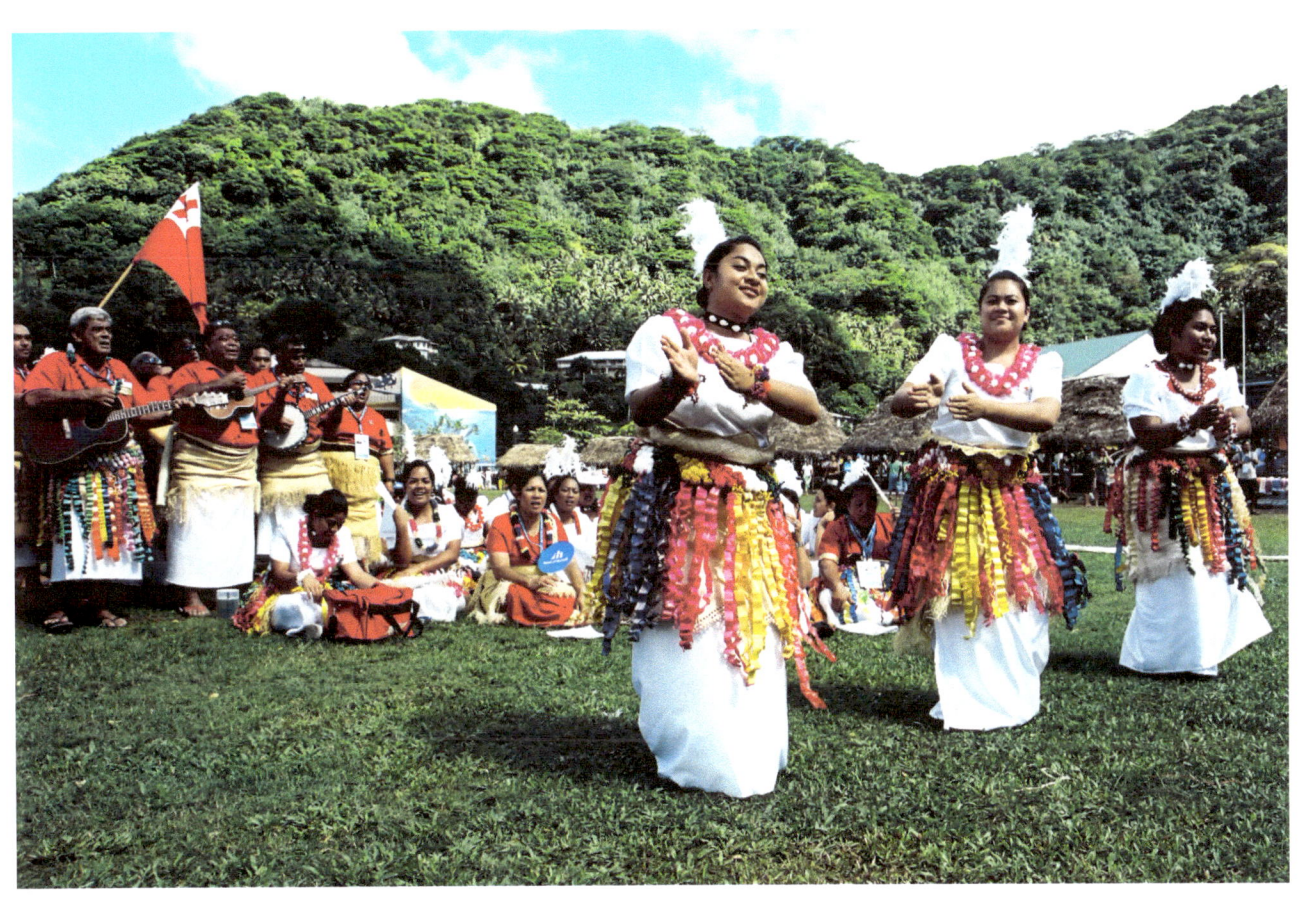

Male dancers from Tonga wore costumes made from Tongan tapa.

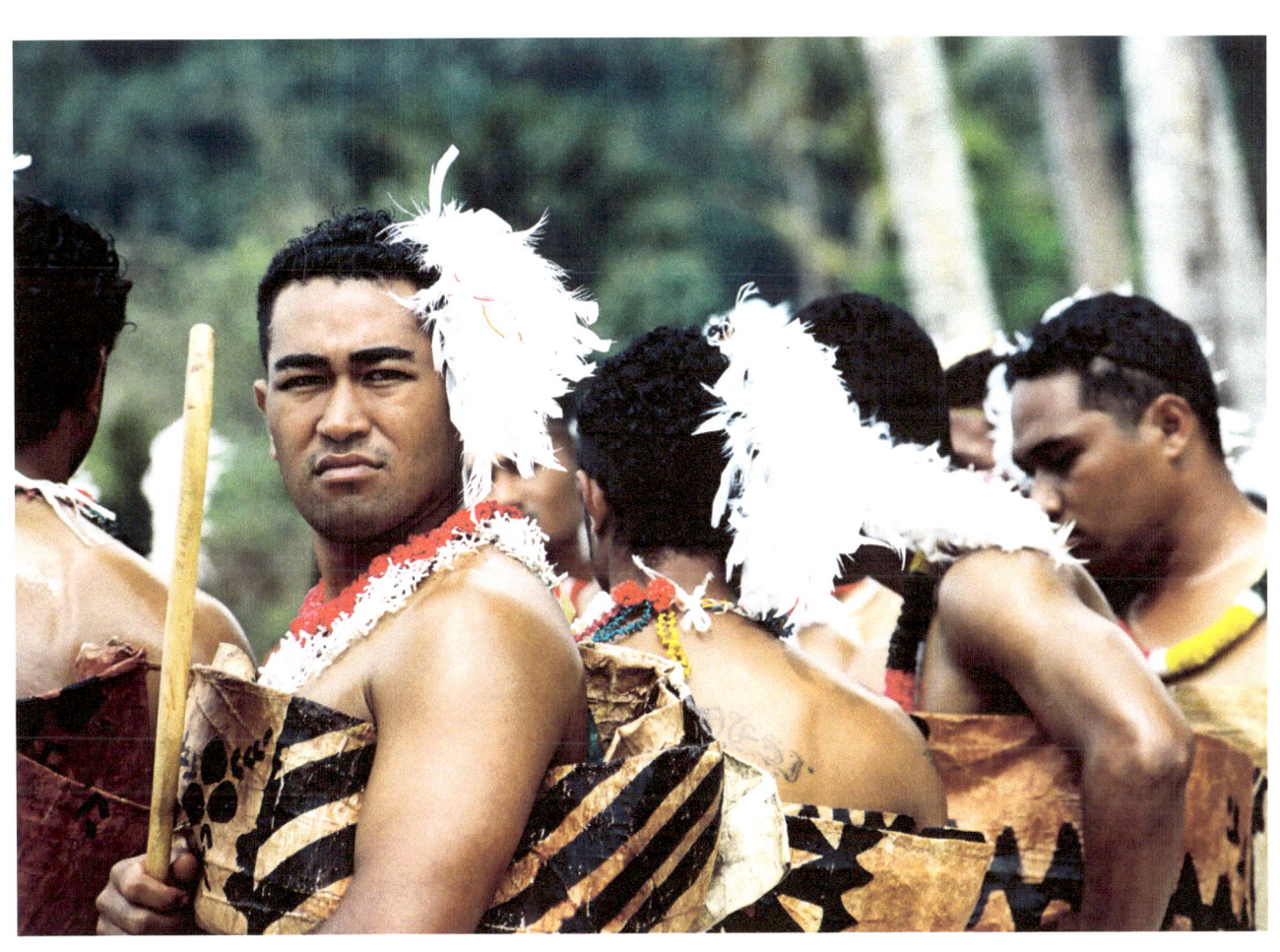

The Festival of Pacific Arts showcased traditional and contemporary fashions by the national delegations. This performer wears traditional attire from New Caledonia.

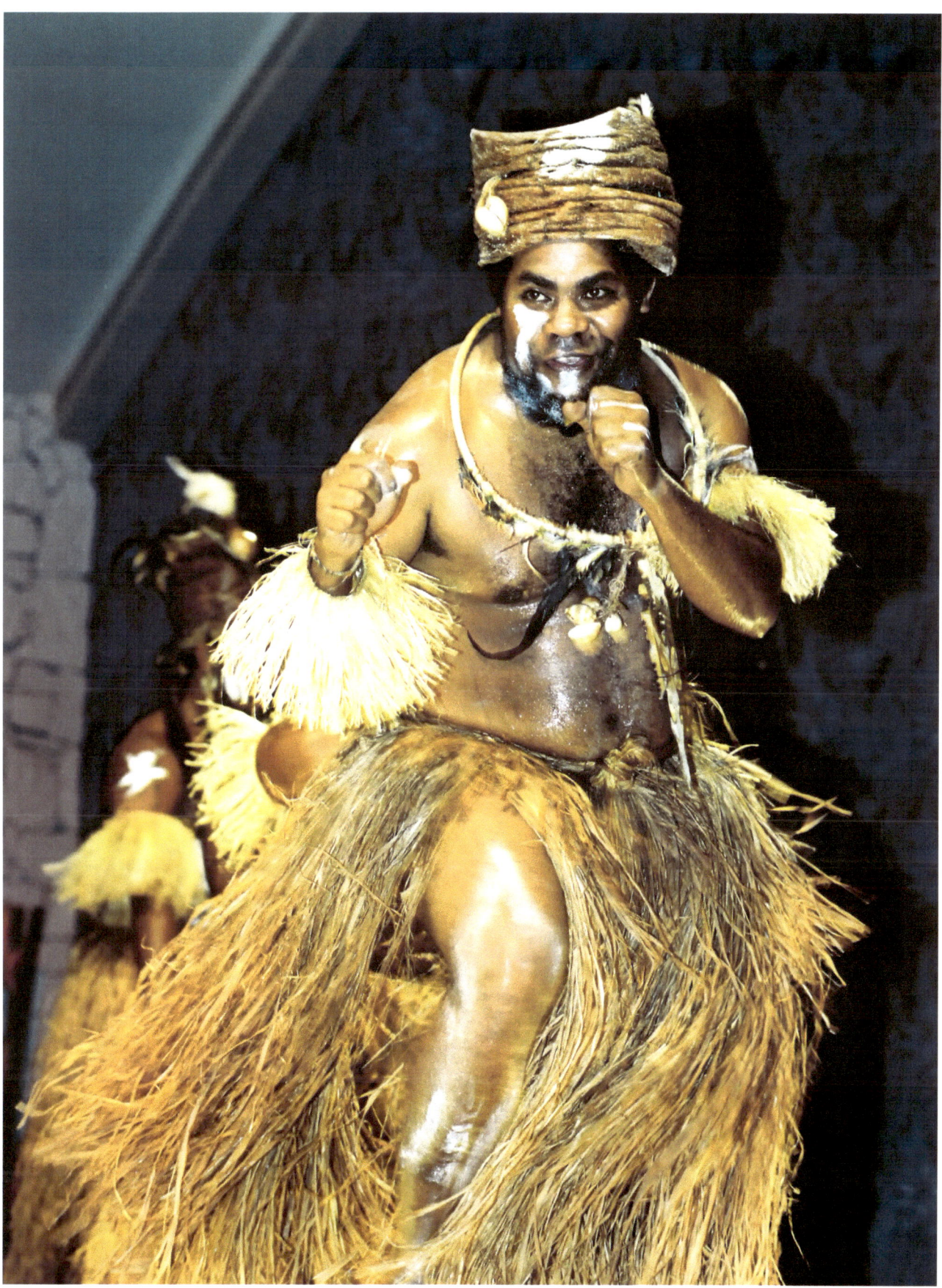

An American Samoan dancer wears a puletasi, a two-piece dress worn in both Samoas.

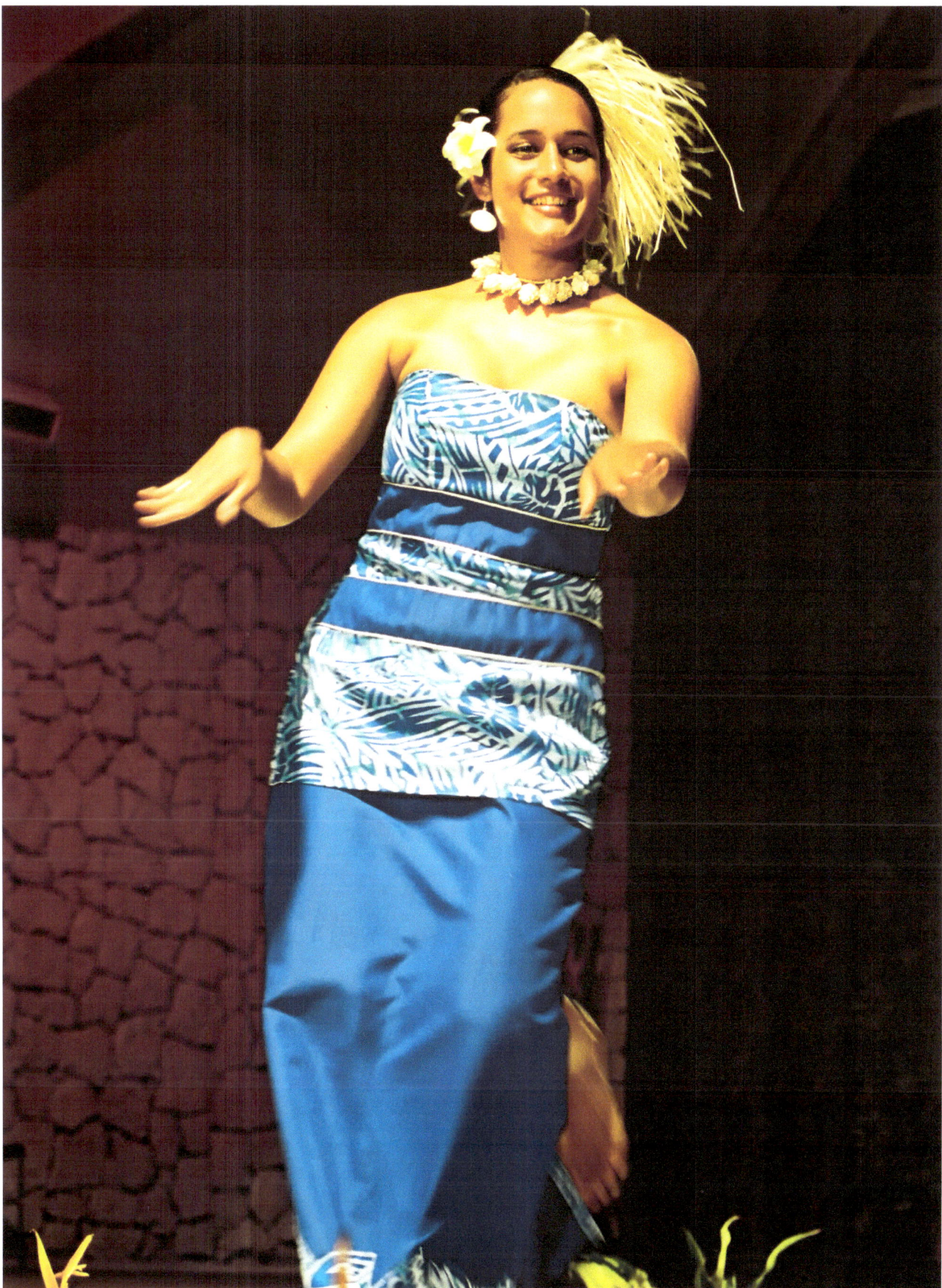

A performer from Tonga sports a contemporary resort-wear dress.

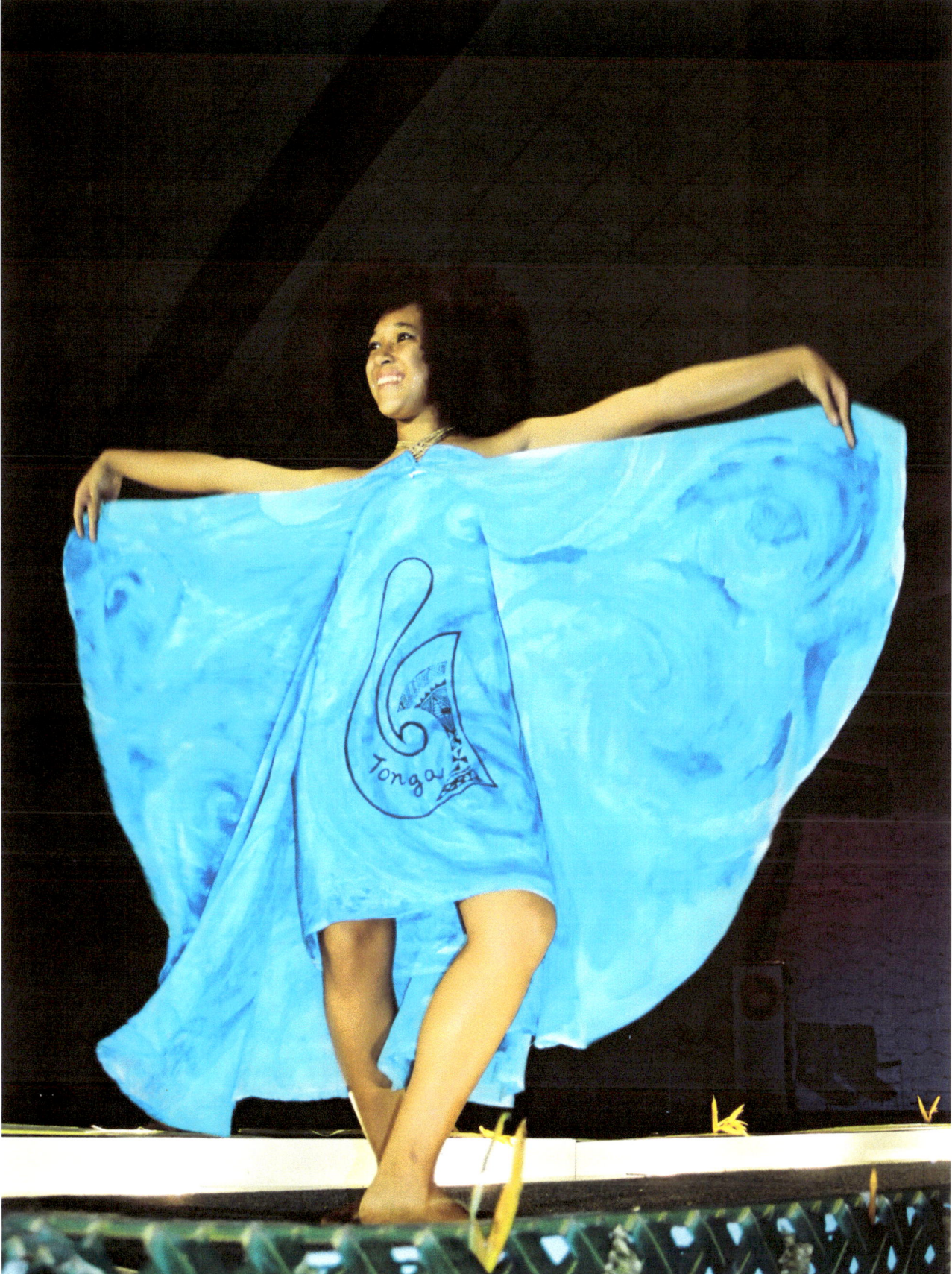

A dancer from American Samoa wears a contemporary interpretation of traditional male attire.

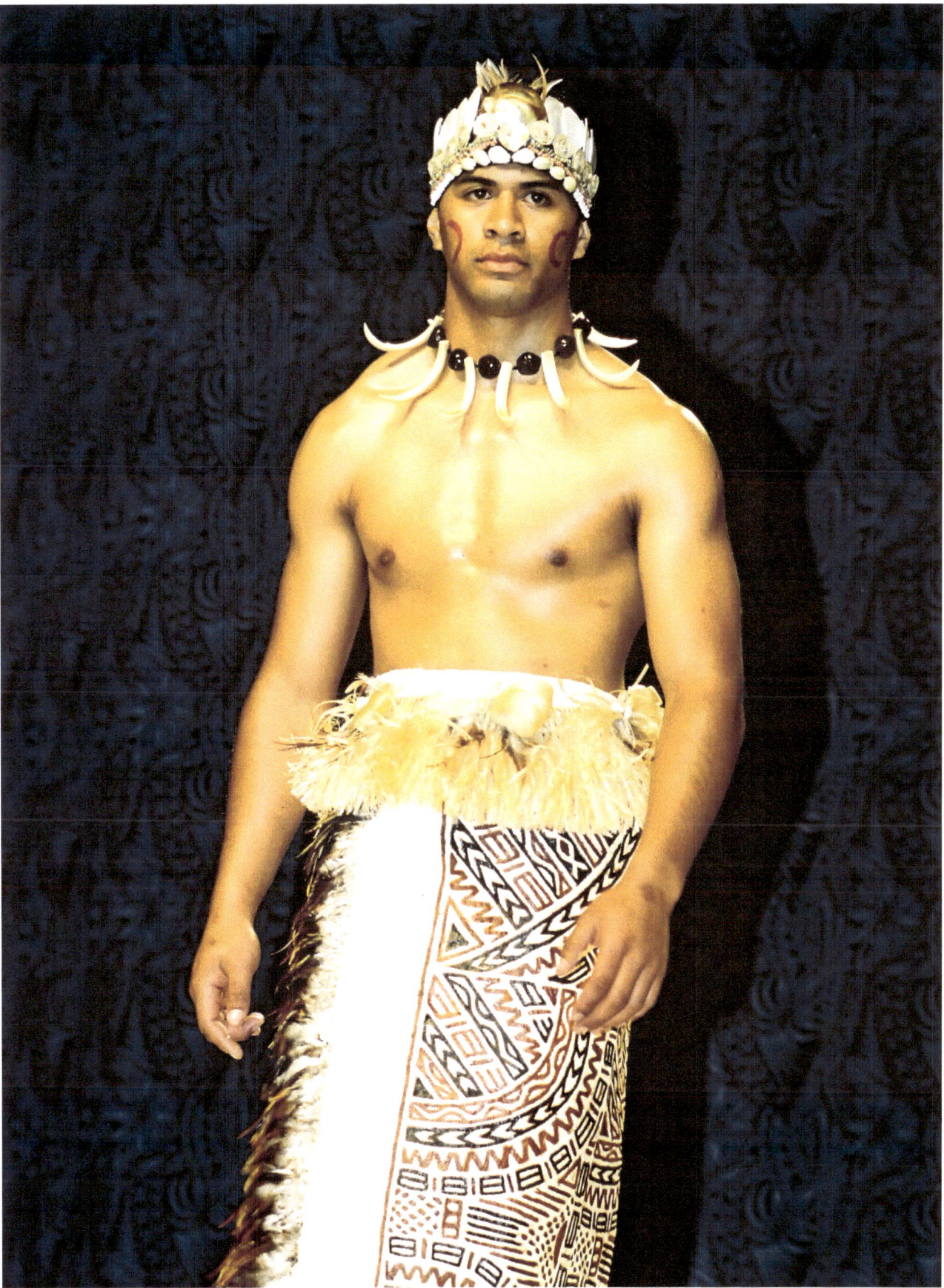

The Festival of Pacific Arts featured a fire-knife dance competition for Samoan participants.

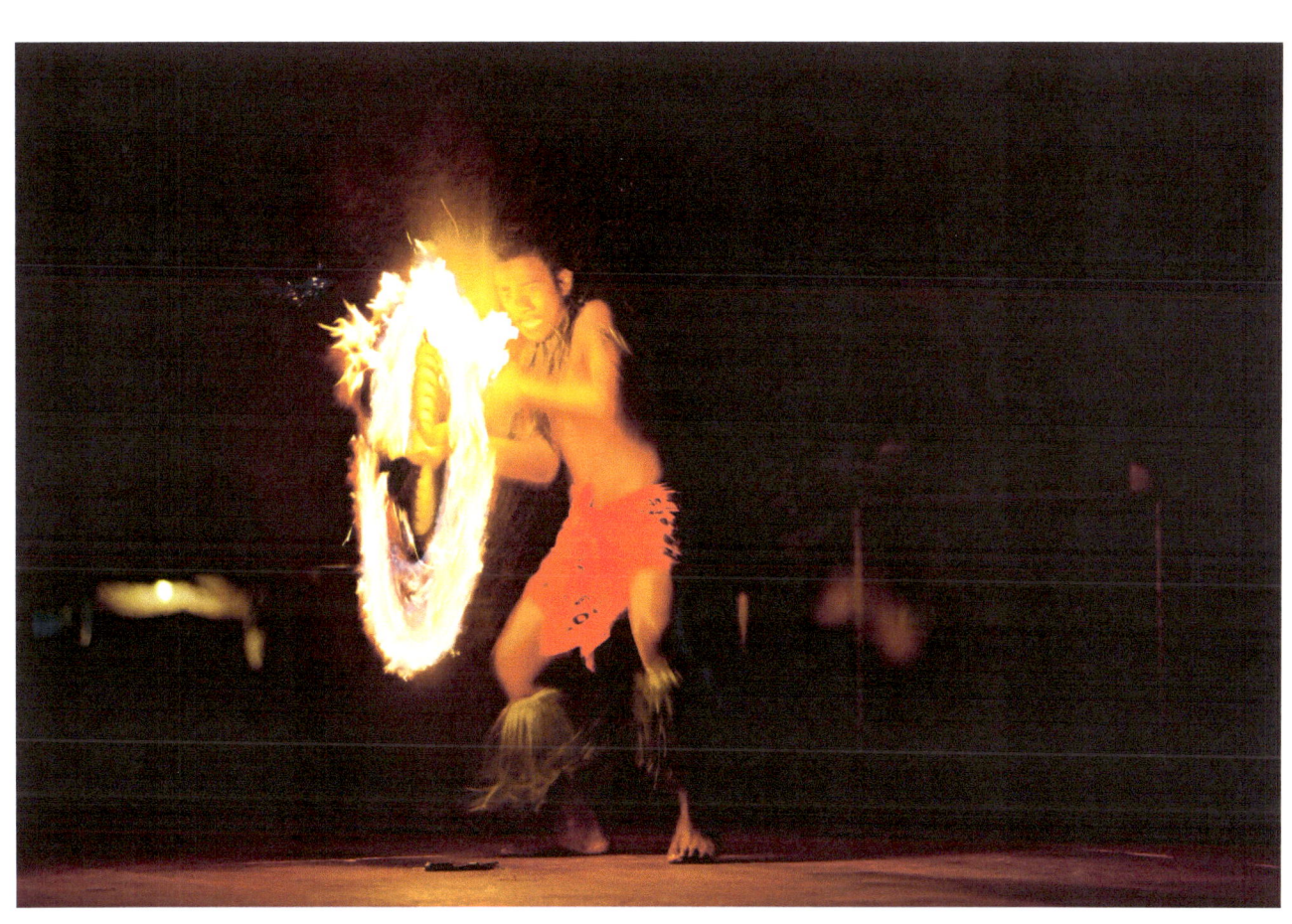

A fast-paced drumbeat helped fire-knife dance competitors move quickly across the stage.

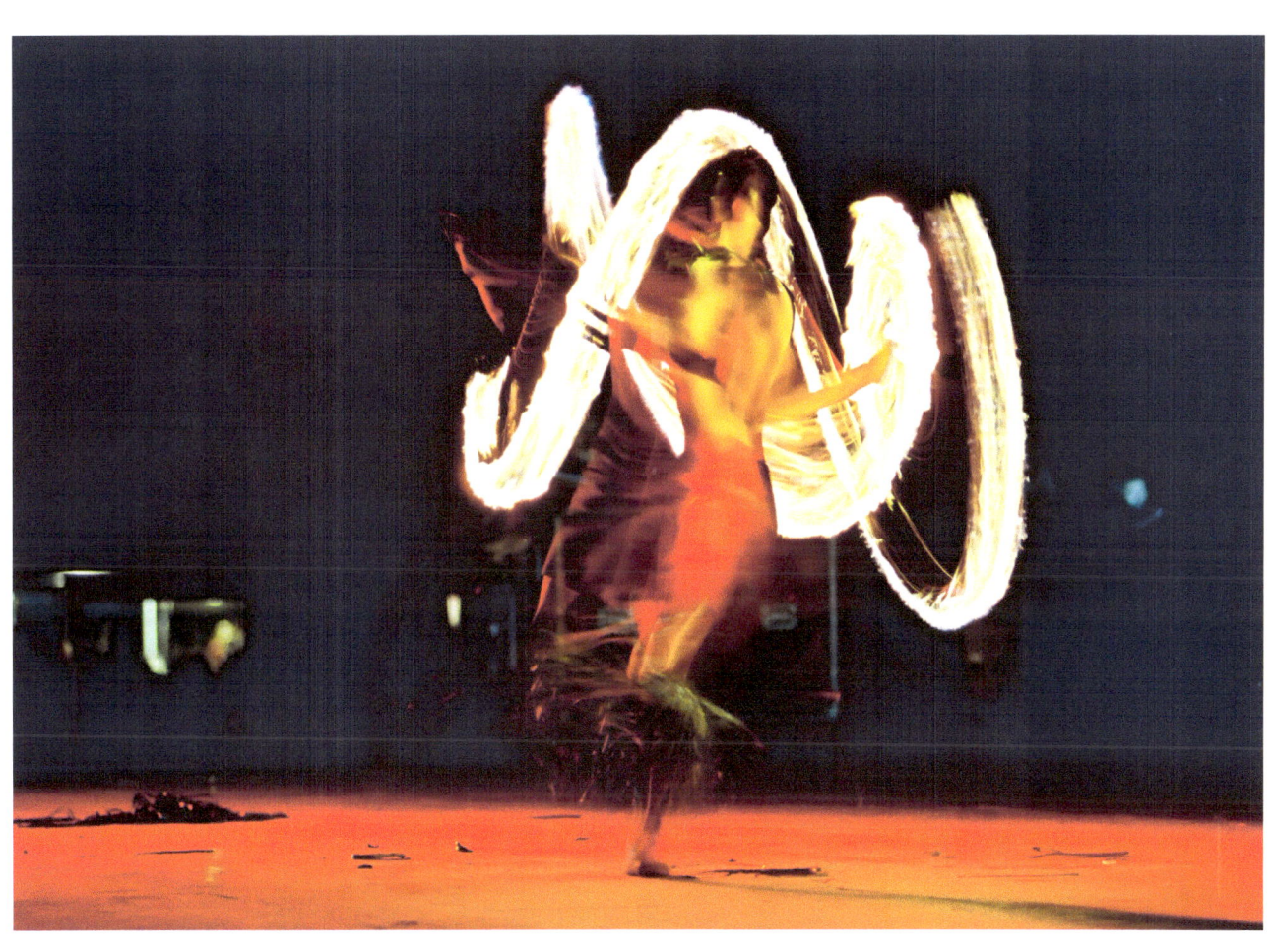

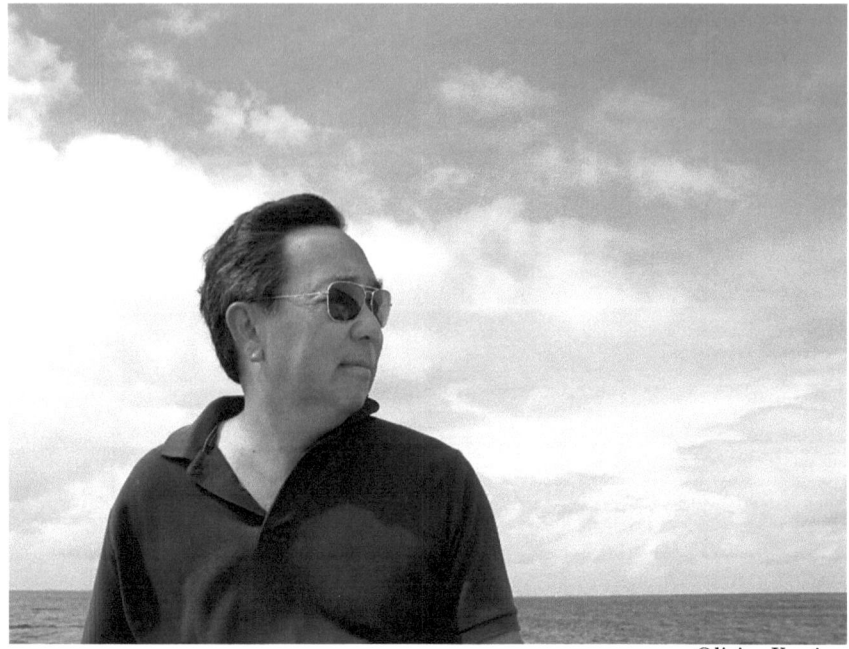

Olivier Koning

The Author

Floyd K. Takeuchi is a writer-photographer who specializes in the Pacific Islands. He has traveled widely in Oceania, and has reported from many of the islands. He has been a resident journalist in Guam, Fiji, Hawaii and Japan, and worked in Washington, D.C. as a senior staffer for a Member of the U.S. House of Representatives. Floyd is co-author of *Majuro – Essays from an Atoll*, and wrote and photographed *School On The Hill, Micronesia's Remarkable Xavier High School*. Both books are available exclusively at Amazon.com. Floyd was born and raised in the Marshall Islands. For more information, please visit www.floydtakeuchi.com.

Thanks and Fa'afetai

More than 30 years of being a journalist in the Pacific Islands, with many thousands of miles of travel on planes and boats, didn't prepare me for the visual riot that is the Festival of Pacific Arts. The 10th Festival, held in American Samoa in mid-2008, was two-weeks of sensory overload, with Oceania's best performers doing what Pacific Islanders do best – sharing with unrestrained joy their rich cultural heritages.

A number of people played important roles in making this project a reality. Oscar Betham, a veteran videographer, was my project partner shooting video for our companion e-book. His delightful mother, Mille Betham, was my surrogate mom in American Samoa. She allowed me to rent her cheery bungalow on the Betham compound in Tafuna village, and made sure that my laundry was done each day. Millie made me a part of the Betham aiga, or family. Fa'afetai!

Long-time friend Barry Rose, a prominent attorney in American Samoa, gave me full run of his law firm, Rose Joneson Vargas. His posh conference room was my office in the territory, and his staff made sure I secured one of the last rental cars available on Tutuila.

Isabel Steffany Hudson, a friend and successful hotelier, extended without hesitation her wonderful Samoan hospitality. She made available her oceanfront Moana O Sina resort for us to shoot a video of the reigning Miss American Samoa, even letting us use her truck's stereo to play the song!

Finally, while I was photographing in American Samoa and turning five shades darker in the tropical sun, my lovely wife, Kris Tanahara, waited patiently for me in Honolulu. Kris is my biggest fan, and I couldn't travel around the Pacific without her love and support.

Floyd K. Takeuchi
Honolulu, Hawaii

www.ingramcontent.com/pod-product-compliance
Lightning Source LLC
Chambersburg PA
CBHW051017180526
45172CB00002B/379